THE TRAINEE TEACHER'S HANDBOOK

Sara Miller McCune founded SAGE Publishing in 1965 to support the dissemination of usable knowledge and educate a global community. SAGE publishes more than 1000 journals and over 800 new books each year, spanning a wide range of subject areas. Our growing selection of library products includes archives, data, case studies and video. SAGE remains majority owned by our founder and after her lifetime will become owned by a charitable trust that secures the company's continued independence.

Los Angeles | London | New Delhi | Singapore | Washington DC | Melbourne

THE TRAINEE TEACHER'S HANDBOOK

A COMPANION FOR INITIAL TEACHER TRAINING

CAROL THOMPSON AND
PETER WOLSTENCROFT

SAGE | Learning Matters

Learning Matters
An imprint of SAGE Publications Ltd
1 Oliver's Yard
55 City Road
London EC1Y 1SP

SAGE Publications Inc.
2455 Teller Road
Thousand Oaks, California 91320

SAGE Publications India Pvt Ltd
B 1/I 1 Mohan Cooperative Industrial Area
Mathura Road
New Delhi 110 044

SAGE Publications Asia-Pacific Pte Ltd
3 Church Street
#10-04 Samsung Hub
Singapore 049483

Editor: Amy Thornton
Development Editor: Jennifer Clark
Production Controller: Chris Marke
Project Management: Deer Park Productions
Marketing Manager: Lorna Patkai
Cover design: Wendy Scott
Typeset by: C&M Digitals (P) Ltd, Chennai, India
Printed in the UK

First published in 2018 by Learning Matters Ltd

Library of Congress Control Number 2017957600

British Library Cataloguing in Publication Data

A catalogue record for this book is available from the British Library.

ISBN 978-1-5264-2399-3 (pbk)
ISBN 978-1-5264-2398-6

Contents

About the authors

Carol Thompson is a Senior Lecturer in Teacher Education at the University of Bedfordshire. She has more than 25 years' experience of teaching and managing learning and is an active researcher, currently dividing her time between research activity (supported by an FETL Fellowship) and the development of teacher education programmes.

Peter Wolstencroft is a Senior Lecturer in Leadership at Coventry University. A firm believer in the transformative power of education, his educational philosophy is that a good teacher should always encourage students to examine the ways in which they see the world and seek out new ways of doing things. An active researcher, his previous work has centred around the day-to-day experiences of those working in education.

Introduction: 'The map is not the territory'

Teaching is a creative, relational role which involves spending whole days talking about your favourite subject! Perhaps naively, when starting teacher training most of us tend to focus on the more attractive aspects of the work but we also need to remember that this is a professional role and as such there are expectations, responsibilities and, very probably, parts of the job you don't enjoy. The same can be said for the experience of teacher training. As a trainee you will be introduced to a world of new knowledge and a range of practical techniques. There will be topics you find fascinating and others you don't. All of this is part of the process of becoming a teacher and all aspects of the training are equally important. It is our belief that having a clear understanding of the role and the skills needed to undertake it will help you to see the relevance in the things you are learning.

During your training, you will be developing technical skills, trying out new things, getting to grips with how theory underpins practice, reading, discussing, analysing and grappling with new ideas. In principle you will be following the same specification as others in your group, at least in terms of the course content and assessment requirements. Yet for each of you the journey will be very different. We have used Alfred Korzybski's well known phrase *the map is not the territory* to illustrate this point. The original usage of this term was to outline the relationship between an object and the representation of that object, but in common usage it refers to the concept that the way we see the world isn't necessarily 'reality'. Likewise, the way you view your training journey will not represent everyone's reality but will be particular to you – and it is up to you to ensure that you get the most out of the experience.

The process of becoming a teacher is quite unique and, as such, there is no single path or direct map to follow. Perhaps the most important thing is that the journey will involve being open to new experiences and being able to reflect honestly on your own skills and abilities. The intention of this book is to help you to do just that and to allow you to personalise your own learning we have included a space to set specific goals for yourself.

We have mapped the content of this book to the Teachers' Standards as well as the Professional Standards for FE and Skills teachers (you will find these in the appendix at the end of the book) but it was never the intention to produce a 'tick-list' book. Instead, our aim is to provide a guide to support you through the important parts of your training, therefore the book is divided into three parts, each exploring a specific aspect of the teacher training journey.

- Part 1 is entitled 'Learning to Teach' and considers the ways in which you can take control of your training by thinking about your core values in relation to teaching as well as the ways in which you can work with the people who will support you on the programme.
- Part 2 is called 'Your Teaching Practice' and has a focus on how you can apply your own learning in the classroom. In this section we will look at some of the key theories alongside the main aspects of the role and will think about teaching strategies, assessment techniques and the ways in which you can create a positive, well-managed classroom.
- Part 3 has a focus on the very important, but often neglected, part of your professional role – 'Continuing Your Learning'. This section considers the wider aspects of the role and the ways that you can get the most out of it.

In each of the chapters we have included relevant theory and examples of how this can be applied to practice. You will also find an 'in a nutshell' feature at the end of every chapter to remind you of key information. Handy printable versions of these features are available to download and print from https://uk.sagepub.com/en-gb/eur/the-trainee-teachers-handbook/book257379. Our experience of using these has been very positive and our students have found them invaluable in the transition between learning about theory to applying it in the classroom.

Starting your teacher training is a very exciting challenge. It won't always be an easy ride and there will be times when you may question what you have taken on, but if you approach it with openness and a sense of adventure if will be one of the most rewarding experiences you have.

We hope your teacher training journey is challenging, fulfilling and, most of all, unique to you. We offer this book as a guide for the journey and, in a sense, it can be seen as a map – but we expect *you* to discover the territory!

Reference

Korzybski, A (1931) *A Non-Aristotelian System and Its Necessity for Rigour in Mathematics and Physics.* Paper presented before the American Mathematical Society at the New Orleans, Louisiana, meeting of the American Association for the Advancement of Science, 28 December 1931. Reprinted in *Science and Sanity* (1933), pp. 747–61.

Part 1

Learning to teach

In this section, you will be discovering the skills you need to make a success of your training. This will help you to plan your journey and use your time effectively.

The following chapters will explore:

- **ways in which you can work effectively with others;**
- **how to use feedback and self-reflection to enhance your development;**
- **strategies for overcoming barriers and developing your resilience.**

1

Why do you want to teach?

In this chapter we will explore:

- **philosophies of teaching;**
- **values, beliefs and attitudes;**
- **skills for teaching.**

Introduction

Our motivations and values have a great influence on how we develop as teachers and establishing these at the outset will help you to plan your professional progress effectively. Although you have already taken the decision to pursue a teaching career, it is important to explore the reasons behind this and in this chapter we will consider the motivations, philosophies and values that underpin these choices.

Why teach?

Before you embark on your journey think about the events which brought you to this point. *Perhaps it was your love of learning? A desire to share your knowledge with others? Maybe you were inspired by one of your own teachers?* Having a clear view of the underlying reasons which fuelled your motivation will help to establish your base philosophy in relation to the role, as well as highlighting your core values, both of which are important to remember when you come across challenges in your career.

Reflection

Imagine you are at your first job interview and are asked the question 'Why did you want to become a teacher?' What would you say? Without spending too much time deliberating (much as would be the case in an interview) jot down your initial thoughts and then come back to these when you have finished reading the chapter.

Your initial answers will tell you something about your *motivation* which, in turn, will influence the sort of teacher you become.

Recent research (Chiony *et al.*, 2017) explored the main things which draw people to the teaching profession and concluded that these were largely based on either intrinsic or altruistic motivations. For many teachers and trainees, the desire to do something they found satisfying which was also socially meaningful was a big draw and reasons such as 'making a difference to others' were cited as key motivators.

For participants in the research, the top five reasons for choosing teaching as a career were as shown in Figure 1.1.

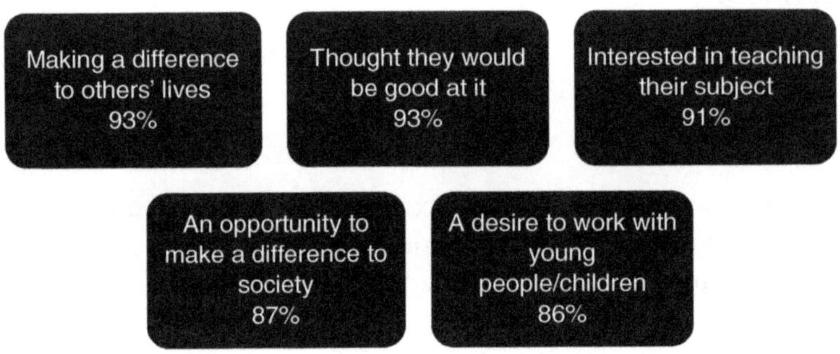

Figure 1.1 Top five reasons for choosing teaching as a career

The research also developed a typology of 'teacher types' and identified four broad categories of teacher which were described as in Table 1.1.

Table 1.1 Typology of teacher types

Practitioners	Teachers motivated by a desire to teach and work with students.
Moderates	Teachers influenced by a broad range of factors.
Idealists	Teachers who want to make a difference to society.
Rationalists	Teachers who weigh up a combination of pragmatic, personal and social justice-related factors.

If you are interested in finding out more about this, or want to take the test (which has the usual limitations associated with remote, online questionnaires), then go to teacherquiz.lkmco.org.

All of this is very interesting and may well resonate with your own reasons for choosing a career in teaching but although these initial motivations are important it is even more important to consider what it is that makes people stay in teaching. This is particularly true at times when the job seems very difficult and we are challenged to remember the reasons why we chose it in the first place.

Some philosophies of education

There are a number of philosophies relating to education which provide us with a starting point in thinking about our views of the purpose of teaching and education overall. These are outlined below to prompt initial thinking about your own philosophies which in turn may lead to a greater understanding of your *values* in relation to education.

Figure 1.2 Perennialism

Perennialism

Perennialism presents a highly determined view of education and sees it as a vehicle for presenting fixed 'truths'. In this sense, educational institutions would exist simply to teach the commonly accepted 'truths' and may do so through a series of structured lessons. It is easy to imagine the advantages of having such certainties in life, particularly in terms of structuring teaching and subsequently learning against pre-determined expectations; likewise it is not difficult to imagine the limitations of this approach. The name itself suggests a degree of conformity and stagnation – like the perennial plant, the conditions in which it will grow remain fixed, as does the plant itself, never having an opportunity to blossom in a way which differs from its predecessors.

Idealism

Idealism is based on the view that reality is individually constructed and that ideas are the only 'true reality' as well as the only thing worth knowing. Plato is considered the 'father' of idealism and he described a utopian society in which the purpose of education was to bring latent ideas to consciousness and discover and develop each individual's abilities. From a teacher's perspective, this would mean a focus on handling ideas through discussion and Socratic dialogue (a method of teaching based on questioning to clarify knowledge). By using these methods, a teacher is eliciting information rather than providing it and becomes a guide as opposed to a sage. While at first glance this might seem very appealing, the reality of a large group of students all having individually constructed realities can be overwhelming.

Realism

Realism is a philosophy based on the belief in the world 'as it is'. In this sense, 'reality' would be based on observations and the scrutiny of observable data. A curriculum based on the principles of this philosophy would emphasise the physical world (in particular disciplines such as science and mathematics) in order to study structure and form and develop rational thinking. The teacher's role in this case would be to organise and present content systematically and use methods which encouraged the mastery of facts and basic skills. As with perennialism this has the advantage of being an organised, systematic approach to teaching, although it may potentially stifle creativity by limiting the scope of teaching and learning to that which is observable and considered factual.

Pragmatism

For pragmatists things are only considered 'real' if they are experienced or observed. From this perspective, there is no absolute because things are always changing so the aim is not to search for 'truth' so much as truth in what works. John Dewey applied this philosophy in his progressive approaches based on the premise that learners must adapt to each other and to their environment, therefore learning would take into account the social experience, the context, place and time. A pragmatist approach to teaching would have a focus on methods which involved hands-on problem-solving, experimentation and working in collaboration.

Figure 1.3 Existentialism

Existentialism

Existentialism is based on the belief that we all have a personal interpretation of the world and this is defined at an individual level. In this sense individuals are defined by the choices they make and not driven by others' views. For Sartre, the existential moment comes when a young person realises for the first time that choice is theirs and they are responsible for themselves so that their question becomes 'Who am I and what should I do?' In relation to education, an existentialist classroom would be one in which choice is paramount and where the teacher emphasises that answers come from within individuals rather than an outside authority. Therefore the educational experience would focus on creating opportunities for self-direction and would start with the individual learner, not the curriculum. At first sight, this seems like a good approach to take in many classrooms and helps develop skills needed by students when they complete their courses; however, in an educational culture driven by the achievement of targets it can be difficult to implement.

Activity

Go back to the beginning of the chapter and look at your answer to the interview question. Now that you have some information about key philosophical approaches to teaching how would you frame your answer? Could you relate to a particular philosophy, or articulate professional values which are important to you?

Skills for teaching

As well as exploring your motivations for teaching it is also worth reflecting on the skills, attributes and personal traits best suited to the task. After all, even the most altruistic motivations will not make up for a mismatch between these characteristics and the requirements of the role.

As outlined by the Department for Education:

> *Teachers make the education of their pupils their first concern, and are accountable for achieving the highest possible standards in work and conduct. Teachers act with honesty and integrity, have strong subject knowledge, keep their knowledge and skills as teachers up-to-date and are self-critical, forge positive professional relationships and work with parents in the best interests of their pupils.*
>
> (Department for Education, 2016, p. 10)

What does this quote tell you about the values and attitudes expected of teachers? The quote was taken from the standards for teachers within primary and secondary settings but is equally relevant in post-compulsory education. What is clear is that teachers are expected to carry out their roles with the utmost professionalism and that requires commitment to personal and professional development from the outset.

Values, beliefs and attitudes

Being aware of our values seems like something which is commonplace and even common sense. But what are values? How do they influence our beliefs, behaviour and attitudes?

Values

Values could be described as the 'guidelines' for how we choose to live our lives. For some people values are based on ingrained beliefs about how life 'should be'; for others they may be strongly influenced by family, peer groups, culture or religion. Values often concern those things that are at the 'core' of life such as personal relationships, social roles and interaction with others. Our core values are the principles which dictate our behaviour and influence our thoughts, so if we want to make any changes to the things we do, or how we do them, understanding our values is a good place to start.

The development of our personal values often starts at an early age and is influenced by parents, family and parental figures. However, these may change as we interact within the wider society and begin to develop our own personal beliefs which are derived from our experiences.

Values and beliefs

Values and beliefs are interconnected: our values could be described as the 'truths' we consider important – for example, integrity, courage, fairness, honesty – and our beliefs are the judgements we make about ourselves and the world around us, often based on the things we consider to be true. In turn, both values and beliefs will influence our attitudes and behaviours.

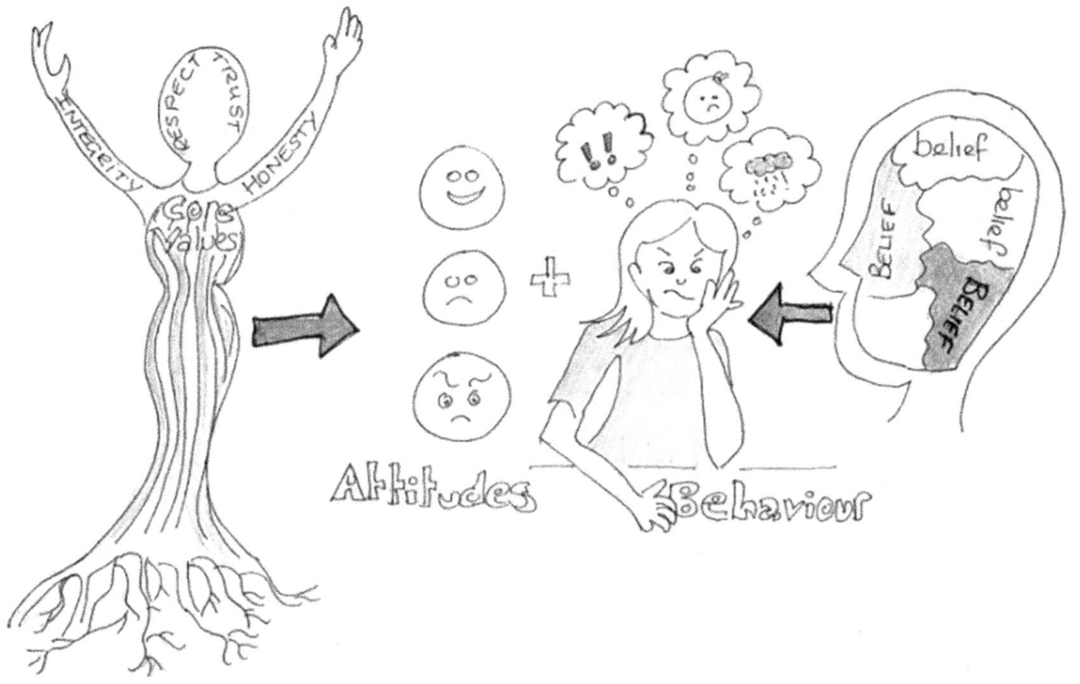

Figure 1.4 Values, behaviours, beliefs

For example, if you believe that teaching is a 'gift', it might be easy to assume that it cannot be learned, therefore any difficulties you come across in your teaching practice might be dismissed as something you cannot do (if you don't have 'the gift'). Conversely, you could also assume that such difficulties are the result of the behaviours of others and therefore your approach need not change. If such beliefs go unexamined we risk limiting ourselves to tried and tested attitudes and behaviours which may not be working for us.

Values, beliefs and behaviours all have an influence on our approach to others and how we conduct ourselves personally and professionally, something which is illustrated by the following quote:

> *Your values become your thoughts,*
>
> *Your thoughts become your words,*
>
> *Your words become your actions,*
>
> *Your actions become your habits,*
>
> *Your habits become your values,*
>
> *Your values become your destiny.*
>
> (Mahatma Gandhi)

In order to meet the requirements of your teacher training course it is important to take responsibility for your own professional development. A good starting point for this is to think about the things you are already confident about and those things which need more development. Table 1.2 provides an outline of the skills required to become a teacher. These are based on the Teachers' Standards which underpin teacher training programmes but are not intended to be a direct checklist against them. Being as honest as you can, and remembering that you are at the very start of your training journey, complete the self-assessment by rating yourself from 'very competent' to 'need development'. This activity should help you to establish useful development goals and there is a template at the end of Chapter 7 that you can use to log these.

Table 1.2 A self-assessment of your professional practice

	Very competent		**Need development**	
Planning lessons/ teaching	I am very confident about this	I am confident but need more practice	I am not confident and need to develop this skill	I have no idea how to do this
Own subject knowledge	I am very confident in my subject knowledge	I am confident but keen to develop this knowledge	I am not confident and need to develop my subject knowledge	I have little confidence in my subject knowledge
Promoting learner progress	I have a good understanding of how to do this	I have some understanding of how to do this	I have limited understanding of how to do this	I have no idea how to do this
Setting high expectations	I am very confident I can do this	I am confident I can do this	I am not confident I can do this	I have no idea how to do this
Managing classroom behaviour	I am very confident about this	I am confident but need more practice	I am not confident and need to develop this skill	I have no idea how to do this
Awareness of wider professional responsibilities	I have a good knowledge of the wider professional role	I have some knowledge of the wider professional role	I have limited knowledge of the wider professional role	I do not know what the wider professional role involves
Assessing learning	I have a good understanding of how to do this	I have some understanding of how to do this	I have limited understanding of how to do this	I have no idea how to do this
Adapting teaching to respond to learners' needs	I am very confident I can do this	I am confident I can do this	I am not confident I can do this	I have no idea how to do this

At this stage, it is important simply to think about the key aspects of the role rather than the actual teaching standards. In time you will become more familiar with the specific standards and can then begin to evidence your skills and knowledge against them.

Some things to consider . . .

Things to think about

This part of the chapter is a prompt for your own reflection and may be a useful starting point for any reflective activities you need to undertake for your course. Is it important to have a philosophy about how you want to approach teaching? If so, how will this influence the type of teacher you become?

When you started reading this chapter you may have had very clear views about why you wanted to become a teacher and accepted these as your own 'truth' about the role. Now, you should have a clearer idea about how your initial motivations, values and beliefs might influence your approach to teaching and it is even possible that you might be questioning your initial views.

Figure 1.5 Balloon man

In a nutshell

This feature covers the essentials of philosophies of education and provides examples of this theory in practice. This resource can be photocopied and used as a revision tool or a prompt for discussion with your peers.

Philosophies of education

Perennialism Sees education as a vehicle for presenting fixed 'truths'. Education is seen as a way of teaching and reinforcing this information.	**Idealism** Sees ideas as being the most important aspect of education, the teacher's role being to develop individual capabilities and ideas. Idealists see the world as it *should* be.
Realism Sees the world as 'it is' and recognises the importance of observation. Sees education as a structured and systematic process used to develop rational thinking.	**Pragmatism** Acknowledges the importance of observation and experience as well as the changing nature of knowledge and advocates experimentation and problem-solving.
Existentialism Has a focus on personal interpretation and choice and advocates an approach which focuses on self-direction.	

Putting it into practice

It is likely that your approach to teaching and learning is influenced by a number of things including your values, your experiences and the way you like learning. It is not suggested that you adopt a particular philosophy but that you recognise the impact your beliefs might have on the approaches you adopt. The following table provides some ideas of teaching strategies matched to each of the philosophies.

Perennialism	Structured lessons Activities to reinforce learning Learning checks
Idealism	Differentiated activities Target setting Unstructured tasks Socratic questioning
Realism	Mastery learning Scaffolding learning Case studies
Pragmatism	Experimentation Problem-solving Group work
Existentialism	Worksheets Choice of activities Use of flipped learning

What else could you do?

Suggestions for further reading

Bailey, R (ed.) (2010) *The Philosophy of Education: An Introduction*. London: Continuum Education.

Blatchford, R (2015) *The Teachers' Standards in the Classroom*. London: Sage.

References

Bailey, R (ed.) (2010) *The Philosophy of Education: An Introduction*. London: Continuum Education.

Chiony, C, Menzies, L and Parameshwaran, M (2017) 'Why do long-serving teachers stay in the teaching profession? Analysing the motivations of teachers with 10 or more years' experience in England', *British Educational Research Journal*, DOI: 10.1002/berj.3302.

https://www.gov.uk/government/uploads/system/uploads/attachment_data/file/301107/Teachers__Standards.pdf (accessed 18 February 2017).

2

Planning your journey through teacher training

In this chapter we will explore:

- **typical training journeys;**
- **how to be a successful student;**
- **managing your time effectively.**

Introduction

You are about to embark on an educational journey like no other. You will be doing all of the usual student activities like reading, writing essays, discussing ideas and getting to grips with new skills but you will also have a range of opportunities to apply all of this learning in a practical sense. It is likely that there will be times when you feel on top of the world and your confidence is brimming and others when you seriously question why you embarked on this journey in the first place. *All these feelings are normal*. Spending a little time planning your training journey is a useful strategy to help you to make the most out of it and while it won't guarantee a smooth ride, it will most certainly help you to overcome the obstacles presented to you. In this chapter we will outline some of the things which are typical on teacher training journeys and will introduce you to strategies which will help you to make the most of the experience.

Learning journeys

Trainee teachers come from all walks of life and as a result have a variety of skills which allow them to take different approaches to their training and the challenges associated with it. It is not possible to provide an exact map of what you will encounter but we can outline some of the ways in which you can make this a positive experience.

Reflection

The following two case studies provide examples of individual experiences of training to be a teacher.

Fiona's story

Fiona left school when she was 16 and got a job in a local bank. She enjoyed the work and decided to enhance her promotion prospects by gaining some secretarial skills. She attended evening classes at the local college and learnt a range of useful office skills which helped her to gain a promotion at the bank. After a few years in a more senior role, she decided that something was missing and investigated other types of study which might interest her. She was thrilled to find a range of opportunities and finally settled on a foundation degree course which she eventually topped up to a degree in English. During this time, Fiona also started an unplanned but welcome family and by the time she graduated she was a 40-year-old mother of two. Although it had been difficult juggling a full-time job, a young family and study, Fiona had thoroughly enjoyed learning and made the decision that it was time to change her career. She searched for something which would present the prospect of using what she had learnt and when she read about teacher training opportunities she knew that she had found it!

Sam's story

Sam had always enjoyed learning. He loved school, excelled during his 'A' levels and throughout his undergraduate studies, finally achieving a first class honours degree from a prestigious university. As a maths specialist, he had a lot of choice of career pathways but, as talking about maths was his passion, Sam felt that a teaching career would be ideal for him. When he was accepted onto a teacher training programme he was very excited about the opportunity to share his knowledge with others. Always a 'bookworm' Sam was really looking forward to reading around another subject and his academic career had demonstrated that he knew how to convey this learning to others. All he had to do was complete another course and he would be able to spend his days talking about maths and inspiring young mathematicians.

Question

Each of our protagonists will be faced with obstacles during their training. What do you think they will be? What skills do you think each person brings to this adventure and how might they be used to overcome the obstacles they are presented with?

Your learning journey

A teacher training course has been compared to a rollercoaster. The highs, often occurring when a lesson goes well, contrast with the lows, when lessons don't go to plan, and students frequently talk about going through numerous emotions within one day. The academic year provides a structure for your learning journey, so we have outlined things which are usually seen as key points within this timeframe.

Figure 2.1 Training journey

September–October

This is a busy time of the year when you have to come to terms with the academic side of the course and the practical aspects of teaching. This is also the time when you will have energy and enthusiasm, so make the most of it by getting into some good habits in both your teaching and your learning. If the course and your teaching starts well, reflect on that and try to highlight specifically what you have done to influence this. Likewise, if your start has been less positive, reflection will help, but also talk to others about their experiences and try to learn from them. In either case do not assume that this is the way it will continue; the route to graduation has many twists and turns and is rarely a straight line from A to B. The key to success is to accept that challenges will present themselves and that you will make mistakes but that you will take ownership of this by enhancing awareness of your own actions and the consequences of those actions. As you get closer towards half term you will start to feel the physical and emotional pressures of the experience and a common trap is to plan to use this holiday to catch up on paperwork and study. By all means use some time in this way but also recognise that you will benefit by taking some time to switch off.

November–December

As you head towards the Christmas holiday you should have established some patterns and routines and started to prepare yourself for the final part of the journey. This can also be a time when there are a number of deadlines to meet so stay strong and allocate time for your academic work as well as for planning your teaching. It is very easy to let the practical side of the experience dominate but remember that both are important. The theories, skills and techniques you are learning on your course are what informs your practice and you should be thinking about the ways in which you can apply these to enhance your professional role.

January–March

There is no avoiding the reality that this period of time is hard work for trainees. Your teaching will be at its most pressured and you will have a number of deadlines to meet. The nights are still dark, the workload heavy and energy levels low. It is at this point that trainees often experience challenges they weren't expecting. Perhaps you have a new placement or are faced with a group you find difficult to manage? If your first teaching experience went smoothly it is very easy to assume that the whole experience will be the same. Be mindful of making assumptions – there may be many reasons why things go well (or not), so it is important to be aware of contexts, attitudes, behaviours and consequences. If you are feeling challenged try to break down the challenge and work out the specific aspects of it. This will allow you to highlight approaches you can try in order to improve the situation. As outlined in Chapter 1, it is important to remember your own values in relation to teaching and allow those to inform your practice.

April–June

Although this is the point when you are meeting final deadlines, the end is in sight so it tends to be a positive time of the year and graduation is just around the corner. This does sound like the end of the journey when in fact it is really just the beginning of another.

Taking control of your journey

To some extent, your route through teacher training is already planned. The curriculum has been designed by those awarding the qualification and the practical elements of the course will be clearly set out. At the outset, you should know what to expect in terms of assessment requirements and

Figure 2.2 Super student

practical teaching activities. Nonetheless you are the one who controls how much you get out of the experience and it is up to you to make sure it is a success. As Mark Twain said, 'the dictionary is the only place where success comes before work', so take control of the journey before it takes control of you.

Being a successful student

Being successful isn't the preserve of just a few individuals, it is something we can all aspire to if we have the right approach. That means we need to focus on what we need to do to be successful, rather than simply hoping that it will be the case. As Edison famously said, 'Genius is 1% inspiration and 99% perspiration.' Based on this advice, it is worth spending some time now doing your 'homework' in order to plan a successful route through your teacher training.

Find out what support is available

At the beginning of your training it is worth taking the time to make yourself familiar with the various support mechanisms available to you. Much of this information will be provided to you at the beginning of your course, so make sure you read through all of the additional information such as course handbooks and student/campus information. Find out where all the important resources/support are located and make sure you sign up for anything that will be helpful, for example study skills workshops, support in preparing presentations, searching for literature or academic referencing. You may be surprised by how much is available but unless you take the time to investigate the potential you may miss out.

Be aware of your strengths and areas for development

Although this seems obvious, sometimes we are blissfully unaware of the things we are good at and a little blind to the skills we need to develop. In order to be successful in your training, establishing your strengths and areas for development is something you need to do at the outset. You can then use this information to plan specific development goals which will help you to achieve the things you want. A quick and easy way to do this is by completing a SWOT analysis. SWOT stands for strengths, weaknesses, opportunities and threats. To carry out an analysis you simply produce a list of things in each of the segments. For example, if you are good at organising your time this would generally be considered a strength as it will allow you to meet assessment deadlines. Alternatively, if you find it difficult planning your time, this might be a weakness. Opportunities are those things which you can utilise to your benefit: for example, working with your peers and your mentor is an opportunity to learn from others and your teaching placements are opportunities to test out your knowledge and skills. Threats are those things which may get in the way of you achieving what you want to achieve – a lot of other demands on your time might be a threat. The point is to be completely honest so that you start out with a clear awareness of things you can utilise to your advantage as well as the things which are potential barriers.

Activity

Think about the skills and abilities you have in relation to successfully completing your teacher training. List each of them in one of the four segments of the SWOT template. If there is anything which you need to address as a result of this activity, make sure you give it priority when you are setting yourself goals.

Figure 2.3 SWOT analysis

Planning goals

It is important to remember that to make the most of your learning you need to personalise it and one way of doing this is by setting yourself development goals or targets. This can seem like an unnecessary additional task but there are a number of research projects which suggest that writing down specific developments has a positive effect on achieving them! According to Locke and Latham (1990) the setting of clear goals has a significant impact on motivation and performance as long as the goals are specific and challenging. One way of ensuring this is the case is by setting SMART targets, an approach which is used frequently within education settings (there is more detailed information on this in Chapter 5).

Thinking about thinking

Although a simplistic definition, 'metacognition' is usually described as 'thinking about thinking'. This refers to higher-order thinking which relates to our learning and includes things like planning how to approach a given task, monitoring our understanding of new learning and evaluating our own progress.

Figure 2.4 Metacognition

A first step is to be aware of which strategies work for us and which don't, reflecting on the effectiveness of the strategies used and refining them as necessary. In other words, if what you are doing isn't working, try something else. There is a range of strategies used to develop metacognitive abilities, including the following.

- **Using relational learning by linking new learning to what we already know.** For example, if you are learning about how to plan a lesson, relate this to other things you plan (a meal, a trip). What do you know about one experience that may be relevant to the other?
- **Asking questions to clarify and reflect on your learning.** The process of putting your immediate thoughts into a question is in itself a useful activity as you have to make some sense of them at this early stage. Asking questions allows us the opportunity to clarify details and start making connections with current learning.
- **Reflecting on your learning experiences and critically analysing any assumptions you might be making.** This can be done through self-questioning. For example, how would I use this learning in a real-life scenario? What examples can I think of related to this learning?
- **Thinking aloud by speaking your thoughts as you complete a difficult task.** If you are working with someone else they may be able to point out any errors in your thinking or throw a new insight into your learning, so if you are working alone, think about getting a 'study buddy' who you can talk through ideas with.

- **Using mnemonics to help remember facts** (this is formula or a rhyme which helps us to remember something). For example, many people are taught to remember the colours of the rainbow by using the mnemonic Richard Of York Gave Battle In Vain (Red, Orange, Yellow, Green, Blue, Indigo, Violet).

Cultivate your curiosity

If you want to acquire 'genius tendencies' this is an essential habit to develop. Curiosity is a fundamental trait in learning and encourages us to take an active rather than a passive approach. A learner with enhanced curiosity is open to new ideas and possibilities and will tend to look beyond what is obvious. This trait in itself encourages a 'deep' as opposed to a 'surface' approach to learning. Deep learning is seen as that which requires higher-order cognitive skills and involves analysing and synthesising information to deepen understanding. In contrast, surface learning is acceptance of information which can be memorised for a given purpose (Marton and Säljö, 1984). Being curious adds a new dimension to your learning and your life – there are always new things to attract the attention and new ideas to play with. If you are not a naturally curious person, developing your curiosity will take a little time and practice and there are some simple suggestions in Figure 2.5.

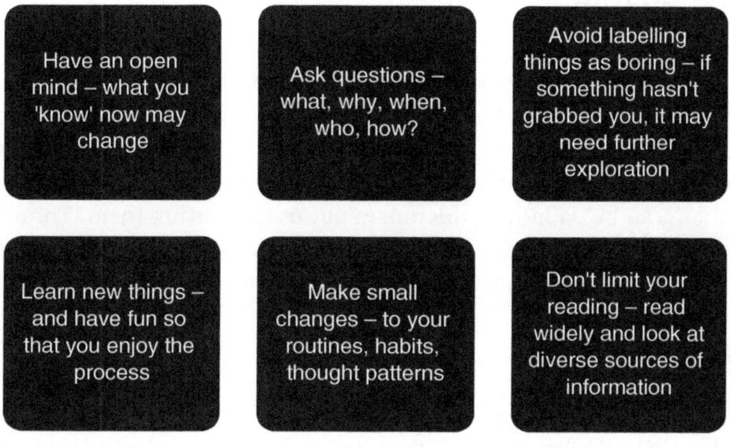

Figure 2.5 Examples of how to develop your curiosity

Managing your time

All of the suggestions in this chapter will be much easier if you are able to manage your time effectively and in this section we will explore a range of strategies which may help. While they may not all work for you, it is worth considering each of them so that you can select the ones that do. Time management is a skill which develops with experience. It takes practice and a consistent approach so it is important that you try things out to find what suits you best.

The starter motor

Just like some cars, some of us struggle to get started on a journey. A survey of students showed that one of the main differences between 'good' students and 'average' students was their ability to get down to work quickly (Butler and Hope, 2007). This in turn can become a strategy for time management. When you have a new task, start it as soon as possible, even if 'starting' is simply planning what you will do.

Ritualising routines

Some routines can become like prisons which stop you from trying new things and curb your creativity, but routine can also help you to manage time. Make routine your friend by creating a ritual out of it. For example, answer emails twice a day for a set amount of time. This way you will not be glued to your computer and get side-tracked from other activities.

Every 'yes' is a 'no' to something else

Saying 'yes' to every opportunity can be tempting but if life is full of commitments there is a tendency to live according to others' priorities rather than our own. When someone asks you to do something, think before you answer and remember that if you say 'yes' to that activity you are saying 'no' to something else.

Elephants near and far

From far away they look small but when they come up close elephants can be very scary. Deadlines are exactly the same. You may have a deadline in three months' time which at the moment doesn't seem like a priority. You know that the work will take four days . . . but you have three months so no rush. In two months, your diary is starting to get full, so you put it off a bit longer; then, before you know it, the deadline is next week and the elephant looks ready to charge. This approach is particularly important for large tasks as these can be daunting which may put us off starting them. Think about how you would approach the task of eating a whole elephant – if you had to do this in one go, it would be overwhelming but if you took things one chunk at a time, eventually the elephant would be consumed.

Use time wisely

Remember you also need time to plan your activities, so make a regular commitment to this, either at the beginning of the day or the beginning of the week. It is also important to be aware of how much of your time is taken up with appointments. For example, if you have arranged to meet a colleague to discuss a joint project, when you arrange a time to meet also arrange a time to finish the meeting.

The curse of perfectionism!

We have all come across colleagues who are sometimes paralysed by their need to produce perfect examples of whatever they do. There is a place for perfectionism but there comes a time when there is not much to be gained from putting in a great deal more effort. Do enough to do a good job – you will know when this is – and then call a halt and focus on something else.

Feeling overwhelmed

A teacher training journey can be quite an emotional experience and there are likely to be times when you feel overwhelmed by all the different demands you have to face. If this happens it is important to talk it through with someone so don't be afraid to approach your tutor or mentor to let them know how you are feeling – both will have been through the experience and will understand. Another strategy you might like to try is putting together an urgency grid. This approach allows you to focus on priorities and on the things that are going to make a difference. In our personal experience it has also been the tool we use to ensure we don't procrastinate when things are becoming overwhelming. By focusing on an urgent and important, followed by an important/not urgent task, you are making sure that key tasks are being tackled and that you are not putting too much energy into the things that matter less.

Activity

To use this approach, start by listing all the things you feel you have to do. Then divide a page into a grid with four categories: important and urgent, important but not urgent, not important but urgent and, finally, not important and not urgent.

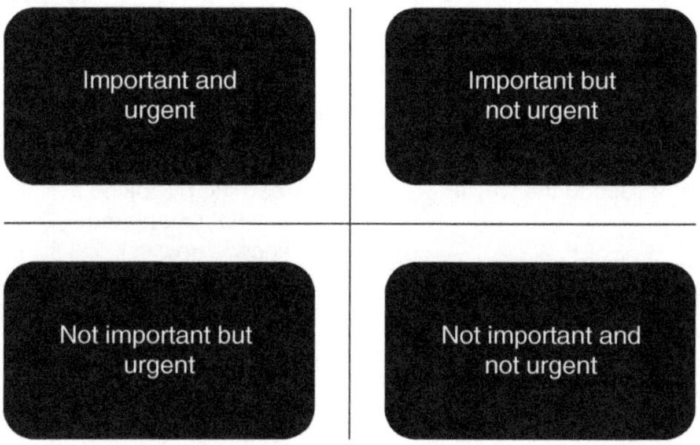

Figure 2.6 The urgency grid

Allocate your activities to the relevant boxes.

- **Important and urgent activities** are usually the things which are easy to identify such as deadlines or feeling prepared for an event but try not to categorise everything in this way - organising your personal files into nice folders and alphabetising them may make you feel better but will it really have a big impact on the outcomes you want to achieve?
- **Important but not urgent activities** are those that help you to achieve your personal and professional goals so you need to make sure you schedule time for these. Including these tasks into your daily routines ensures that you keep on track and reduce the stress of having a lot of last-minute things to do.
- **Not important but urgent** describes the things that often prevent you from achieving your goals and you need to ask yourself whether or not they are things you really need to do. Can they be delegated or rescheduled?
- **Not important and not urgent activities** are usually distractions - they may be things other people want you to do or simply habits you have fallen into.

Things to think about

This chapter is intended to help you to take control of your training journey by highlighting potential barriers to your success and outlining strategies to overcome them. Think about the hurdles that may present themselves to you. Is there anything in your day-to-day life which you need to consider in planning? Are there habits and relationships that challenge you? What strategies can you put in place at the outset to ensure that when obstacles do present themselves you are ready to face them?

In a nutshell

This resource can be photocopied and used as a revision tool or a prompt for discussion with your peers. It is designed to help you when planning your journey through teacher training.

Deep and surface learning

The difference between deep and surface learning is based on two things: first the approach to learning and second the way in which learning is used.

Deep learning is conceptualised as learning which is critically analysed and synthesised by way of linking new concepts to old. A 'deep learning' approach is likely to involve:

- relating new ideas to previous knowledge and experience;
- discovering the key principles which allow the linking of concepts;
- critically analysing information;
- interacting with the learning.

Surface learning might be described as a pragmatic approach in that it is focused on the end result rather than the learning itself. As a result 'surface learners' tend to:

- accept information passively;
- reproduce content;
- focus on assessments;
- memorise facts and routines.

Source: Marton and Säljö (1984).

Putting it into practice

- Question new learning by linking it to what you already know – how is it similar/different?
- Talk about learning with others. Listen to their perspectives and ideas.
- Look for connections – how does one aspect of learning relate to another?
- Think about ways you might adapt a new theory or concept.
- Teach others – if someone else doesn't understand something find a way of making it clear to them.
- Map it – create a concept map outlining all the elements of what you have learnt.

What else could you do?

Suggestions for further reading

Kottler, JA and Kottler, E (2013) *The Teacher's Journey – The Human Dimensions*. London: Corwin.

References

Butler, G and Hope, T (2007) *Manage Your Mind: The Mental Fitness Guide*, 2nd edn. Oxford: Oxford University Press.

Locke, EA and Latham, GP (1990) *A Theory of Goal Setting and Task Performance*. Englewood Cliffs, NJ: Prentice Hall.

Marton, F and Säljö, R (1984) 'Approaches to learning', in F Marton, D Hounsell and N Entwistle (eds), *The Experience of Learning*. Edinburgh: Scottish Academic Press.

3

Working with tutors and mentors

In this chapter we will explore:

- **how to get the most out of working with others;**
- **ways of developing a growth mindset.**

Introduction

In order to get the most out of your training it is important to think about how to work with the people who are there to support you. For most trainees, there are three groups of people who have a significant impact on your success, these are:

- your tutors;
- your mentors;
- your peers.

While it is highly probable that you will establish a way of working with your peers early on in the programme, the most effective ways of working with tutors and mentors might require a little more consideration and getting your approach right at the outset will help you in achieving your goals.

Getting the most out of working with others

Working with your tutor

Your tutor is responsible for providing learning opportunities which will help you develop the knowledge and skills required to become a teacher. They will have a good understanding of the overall programme and be able to explain the relevance of its component parts as well as how they fit together. Tutors are normally the first point of contact if you have questions about course requirements and assessments and they will provide all of the information you need to successfully achieve your goals. In this sense tutors are one of the best sources of support you have access to. However, it is important to remember that they are responsible for a whole group of people, all of whom have different needs and will not necessarily be aware of the best way to support you. For this reason, you should think about ways in which you can help them to do this.

Reflection

Try to put yourself in your tutor's shoes:

- What would you want to know about your students?
- What would you want your students to do if they didn't understand something?
- In what ways would you expect to help students?
- What skills and traits would you like your students to develop?

Also bear in mind that your tutors are not mind readers – in order to get the most focused support, you need to talk to them if you have any questions or concerns.

Activity

Make sure you are familiar with the course requirements and your entitlements by getting to know all of the relevant documentation.

- Read through the course handbook and any course literature.
- Make a list of any questions you have.
- Check how tutorials and additional support are organised so that you know where and who to go to if you need help.
- Look at the university's website to see if there are any central sources of support that may be of use (for example help with study skills).

Working with your mentor

Mentors are a key part of the teacher training journey. They are usually the first people you would talk to about the practical parts of teaching. Mentors may work in the same department as you and are the closest connection between you and the students you are working with. Your mentor is also the person you will see most frequently in your teaching practice.

The mentor's role is to be both a role model and guide. The mentor is the person you will discuss teaching approaches with as well as any concerns you might have about teaching. In simple terms, the mentor's role is to support and nurture but mentors are also expected to challenge and in this way they become a 'critical friend'. The model shown in Figure 3.1 outlines the ways in which mentors help to support development.

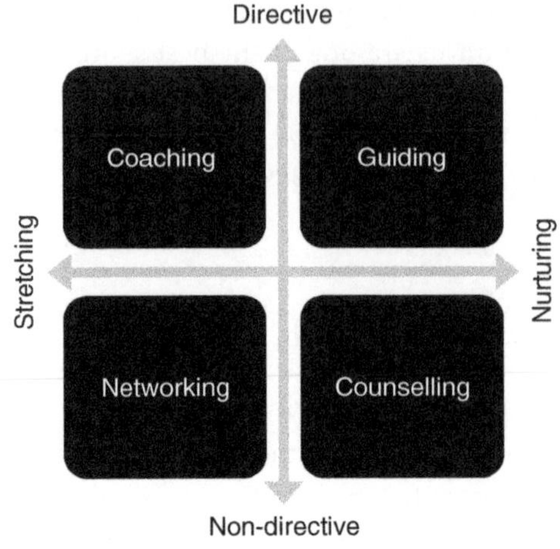

Figure 3.1 Clutterbuck model

Adapted from Clutterbuck (2004).

As you can see from Figure 3.1, the mentor's role is both directive and non-directive. This means your mentor will provide you with very clear guidance and support in some instances and may do this using coaching/guiding techniques; in other situations your mentor will be less directive and may try to get you to find solutions by using techniques such as focused questioning. The role is multifaceted and is one which must be adapted in order to work effectively with each individual. For you to get the most out of this relationship you need find ways of working with your mentor from the very start – anything else would be a waste of precious time and a missed opportunity. The following tips may help you to get started.

- Arrange an early meeting with your mentor and formalise an agreement on how you might work together. There may well be a template in the course documentation but if not you can draw up something simple to work with. This would normally be agreeing things like when and how you will meet, expectations each will have of the other, the best way you can work effectively.
- Ask your mentor if you can shadow some of their lessons so that you can observe their teaching.
- Ask if your mentor could arrange for you to observe another teacher, preferably someone who teaches a different subject, so that you can compare approaches to teaching.
- Talk to your mentor about your reflections on teaching. More than likely they will have experienced the things you are going through and will be able to offer clear advice.
- Ask you mentor for ideas about where you can find appropriate teaching resources – they may well know of things that will be useful to you.
- Listen carefully to any feedback your mentor gives you and discuss ways in which you could act on this feedback.
- Linked to the point above, use your mentor's feedback to develop SMART targets to help you develop specific skills.

Figure 3.2 Targets

- Don't be afraid to ask for support, to discuss concerns and to accept guidance. Mentors are well aware of the challenges you will be facing, after all they have gone through the same process themselves. They won't necessarily be able to 'fix' problems but it is very likely that they can share experiences and offer guidance which will enable you to do this for yourself.

If you help your mentor to support you in the right way, this will be one of the most rewarding parts of your journey as you have the luxury of working with someone whose main focus is to help you to be the best teacher you can be.

Developing a growth mindset

While there are many people who will support you in your training, it is worth remembering that the person who will have the most impact is **you**! Your approach to the experience can be the difference between success and failure and one thing which will have a significant influence is your mindset throughout the training (and beyond).

Mindset is a term used to describe individual approaches to achievement and is based on the work of Carol Dweck (2008) as a result of her research into achievement and success. Dweck suggests that success has more to do with our approach to something than our innate talents or abilities and outlines the difference between a 'fixed mindset' in which people believe that their intelligence, qualities and talents are fixed and a 'growth mindset' in which there is a belief that abilities can be developed through dedication and hard work. This work has had a huge influence on classrooms around the world as it provides a powerful insight into the importance of attitude and motivation.

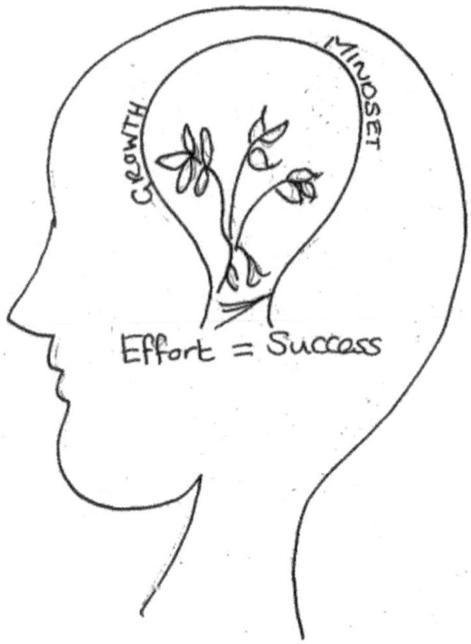

Figure 3.3 Growth mindset

It is possible to consider mindset as some sort of panacea or magic wand, in that all we have to do is *believe* we can do things, apply ourselves to the tasks in hand and, as if by magic, we will be successful, but it is worth remembering that developing a growth mindset isn't just about our efforts – this is a common misconception. Of course, effort and the desire to achieve is important but it is not the only important factor. It is also important to try out new strategies and seek guidance from others when we are stuck on something, if we don't we will simply be expending more effort by doing more of the same thing. Dweck also points out that we should remember that effort is a means to an end, it should be focused in order to achieve a specific learning goal, so simply trying our best isn't enough. Remember, if what you are doing isn't working then you need to try something else. The growth mindset was developed to help close achievement gaps and therefore must include acknowledging the truth about current achievement as well as considering different strategies to reach intended goals.

So how do you develop a growth mindset? Well, according to Dweck, one starting point is to acknowledge that we are all a mixture of fixed and growth mindsets and in order to move closer to a growth mindset we need to recognise the things which trigger certain reactions. A starting point would be to think about the things that are 'triggers' for you. What do you do when you face challenges? Do you feel anxious or perhaps try to move away from the situation? Or do you fling yourself headlong into it, regardless of whether or not you know what to do? Consider the following activity and try to be completely honest about how you think you would respond.

Figure 3.4 Magic wand

Activity

You are really struggling with the group you are teaching at the moment. You have tried a number of ways of getting their attention when you want to explain something but nothing seems to work. The students just carry on chatting to each other and talk over you.

How do you feel about this?

What do you think is happening?

Your immediate reactions to the above scenario may tell you about your mindset, for example if you feel that you cannot control the group because of your lack of authority or because of some fault with the students, then you are probably approaching this with a fixed mindset. If, on the other hand, you recognise that there might be other ways of approaching the task of classroom control and are excited by the challenge of finding the right approach, then you are probably approaching this with a growth mindset. However, the important thing to remember is that it is not about categorising behaviours but is about accepting the current situation and being open to different behaviours which may bring about change. According to Dweck:

> *If parents were to give their children a gift, the best thing they could do is to teach their children to love challenges, be intrigued by mistakes, enjoy effort, and keep on learning. That way, their children don't have to be slaves of praise. They will have a lifelong way to build and repair their confidence.*
>
> (Dweck 2008: 177)

Things to think about

The focus of this chapter is on finding the best ways of working with others in order to achieve your goals. Think about the ways in which this will influence your development and why it is important to establish productive professional relationships. Within this chapter we have also considered the importance of mindset and you should now have a clear idea about how essential this is in successfully completing your studies as well as in developing your knowledge and skills when you are qualified.

In a nutshell

This resource can be photocopied and used as a revision tool or a prompt for discussion with your peers.

Growth mindset

Mindset describes individual approaches to achievement and can be a powerful driver of attitude and motivation. Dweck (2008) describes two mindsets which influence our behaviours and approaches to tasks:

My intelligence and abilities are fixed. There is nothing I can do about that. These will influence my chances of success.

I have certain abilities and talents but can apply myself to tasks in ways which will help me to develop and achieve my goals.

Source: Dweck (2008).

Putting it into practice

There is a variety of ways in which you can develop a growth mindset – the following may be helpful.

- Create space for new ideas – avoid being 'blocked' by what you have always done.
- Make use of formative feedback. Ask for this wherever possible.
- Build time for self-reflection. Keep a journal and look out for repeating patterns.
- Think about ways in which you can do things differently and try things out.

Recognise that you have choices.

Suggestions for further reading

Dweck, C (2006) *Mindset: The New Psychology of Success*. New York: Random House.

References

Clutterbuck, D (2004) *Everyone Needs a Mentor: Fostering Talent in Your Organisation*. London: CIPD.

Dweck, CS (2008) *Mindset: The New Psychology of Success*. New York: Ballantine.

4

Reflecting on your practice

In this chapter we will explore:

- **models of reflection;**
- **ways of recording reflection;**
- **strategies for using reflections effectively.**

Introduction

The idea of reflection has been around for a long time. According to Dewey (1933) reflection is one of the three main ways in which we acquire knowledge and Schön (1983) refers to learning as reflective practice. On this basis it would be reasonable to assume that reflection and learning might be closely connected.

What is reflective practice?

In general, reflective practice is seen as the process of learning from experiences in ways which develop new insights about ourselves or our practice. Through reflective practice we are enhancing self-awareness and critically examining our assumptions and responses to events. The purpose is to recapture experiences and think about them objectively in order to gain new understandings and so improve future teaching. This is articulated clearly by Schön, who describes the process as: 'A dialogue of thinking and doing through which I become more skilful' (Schön, 1983: 31). If we take this as a starting point, our reflections can be seen as a 'stepping stone' in that they provide us with an opportunity to continue our professional and personal development.

Reflection is about our individual learning but for professionals working closely with others it goes a step further. For anyone working in a professional context this is an important activity as the very nature of professionalism is embodied by a number of characteristics such as honesty, integrity and self-regulation. If we choose teaching as a career we should be prepared to show and record that learning and in doing so provide evidence of continual development which will benefit ourselves and our learners. You can start this process now by completing the following activity.

Figure 4.1 Light bulb

Activity

Think about your teaching over the past week and select one lesson to focus on. Write down your immediate responses to the following questions.

- What happened?
- What went well in the lesson?
- What could have been better?
- What would you like to try if you taught this lesson again?

In the activity above you carried out a pragmatic approach to reflection and by answering the questions thought about your practice in a structured way. We will now explore a few models of reflection which may provide a little more depth to the process.

Models of reflection

In this section we will introduce you to some popular models of reflection but we do so with a caveat. Reflection is a personal thing and it is important to develop your own approach to it – after all, you have to find something that becomes a useful activity and an instructive, rather than destructive, habit. So, alongside the models we will consider some practical strategies you can try out.

A popular model is that produced by Gibbs (1988) which includes six stages as shown in Figure 4.2.

Figure 4.2 Gibbs' reflective cycle

This model is sometimes described as an iterative model, which means learning through repetition. For this reason the cycle element is crucial. It is important to think about how each change affects your practice. The aims of the model are to challenge assumptions about the ways we are doing things and consider new approaches where appropriate.

Within Gibbs' reflective cycle the focus is on learning from experience. The approach involves analysing a particular situation in an objective way and provides an opportunity to ask ourselves questions which will generate constructive reflection. The first stage involves describing the situation. At this point it is important to take a step back from what happened, as if you were an observer of the situation rather than a participant in it. This might involve asking yourself questions such as:

Where and when did this happen?

Who else was part of the event?

What happened?

What did I do?

What did others do?

What was the outcome?

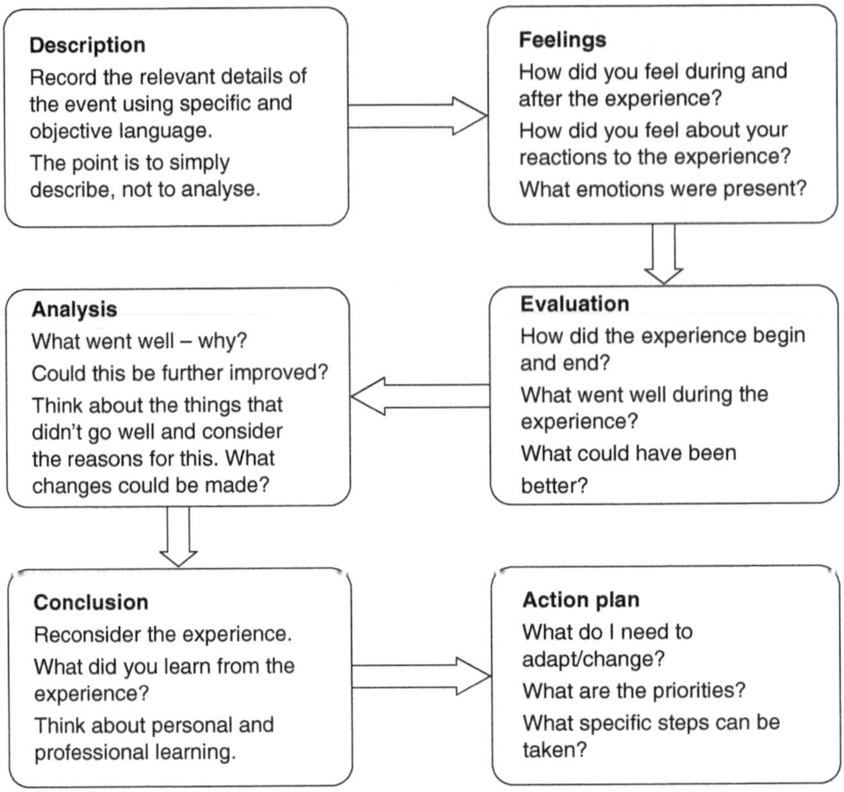

Figure 4.3 Gibbs' reflective cycle in action

Taking this approach might seem overly detailed but by recording such details you are removing yourself from the picture and can note details which you might otherwise miss. In practice this might work as shown in Figure 4.3.

An alternative model is provided by Brookfield (1995), who suggests that reflection is enhanced by applying 'critical lenses' through which we review a teaching and learning experience. These lenses are:

- our own view;
- the view of our students;
- that of our fellow professionals; and
- theoretical perspectives.

Although it could be argued that our own view may be subjective, Brookfield believes that this aspect is one of the most important for viewing the idiosyncrasies of teaching. This is balanced by examining that experience as a learner and with input from other professionals providing a range of perspectives on a given experience as well as the potential for new insights.

Kirkpatrick (1976) developed an evaluation model of reflection which can be directly linked to the teaching and learning context. This consists of four steps as shown in Figure 4.5.

Figure 4.4 Brookfield

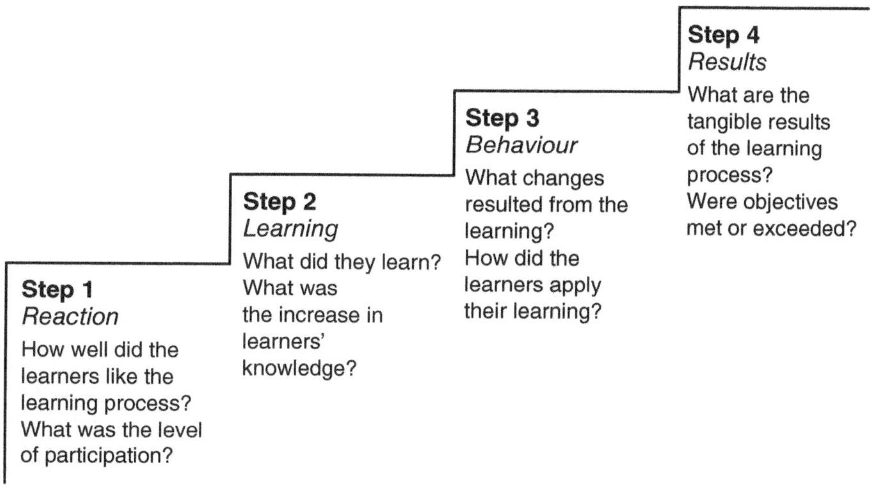

Figure 4.5 Kirkpatrick's evaluative model of reflection

Using models of reflection

Models of reflection can provide a useful starting point when you begin the process of reflective practice. They can act as a prompt or guide and offer a sequential process to follow which allows you to look at experiences in different ways. However, there are also some disadvantages to following any particular model. Models of reflection, in the same way as models of teaching, can create a rather formulaic approach which may mean you miss out on important parts of the activity. For example, the evaluative model proposed by Kirkpatrick does not specifically ask us to think about potential improvements and the model proposed by Brookfield does not take into account the context within which we are working.

As you become more familiar with the process of reflection you should be able to develop an approach that works for you. Remember that you do not have to slavishly follow the prompts in the model – you can simply use them as a guide.

What should you be reflecting on?

Reflecting on our practice seems like an important activity, but where should you start? If reflection is to be used as a 'specialised' form of thinking then it might be useful to consider where we want to focus our thinking. One option is to reflect on those things which could be described as 'critical incidents'. A critical incident is anything in our professional life that has special significance for us, for example:

- being unprepared to deal with a problem that arose;
- something that causes a disturbance of equilibrium;
- a dilemma;
- something that can be seen to have led to a lasting change in professional behaviour, principles or perceptions.

The use of the word 'critical' may be misleading here. It does not necessarily relate to something that has life or death implications; it is simply something we interpret as a problem or challenge rather than a routine occurrence. For example, you may have noticed that learners often talk over each other in class or do not listen to instructions. These things, while not critical in the true sense of the word, will certainly disturb the equilibrium of a positive classroom environment.

Activity

The following excerpt is taken from a trainee teacher's reflective journal. Read through it and then select one of the reflective models mentioned in this chapter. Link the journal entry to stages of the selected model.

> *I'm not sure how nervous I looked or if the students were more aware of my nerves than anything I was saying. I'm not sure I made myself clear or that they understood me. Sometimes I think I need to relax a bit instead of dragging the lesson along. I talked to the whiteboard a lot – always seem to forget that one. It's very difficult to tell if they are listening or if they even care about what I am saying! I suppose at the end of the day there is nothing I can do to make them pay attention or write things down.*

Does the use of the model change the reflection? Does it help you to focus the reflection in a useful way?

Recording reflection

As discussed earlier in the chapter, reflection provides us with an opportunity to carry out an objective examination of professional practice – in effect it is 'witnessing' our own experiences so that we can consider them in more detail. The key to doing this effectively is trying to be as objective as possible. One way to formalise the process of reflection is by keeping a reflective journal and there are a number of ways you can do this. The important thing is to select something which appeals to you and which can be easily worked into your day-to-day activities. Table 4.1 provides some suggestions for potential formats.

Table 4.1 Suggestions for methods of reflection

Questions	**Suggestions**
Do you enjoy writing?	Find a nice, hardback book that you can carry around with you and write whenever you feel inspired.
Do you find it difficult to get started?	Try starting with a template based on/or adapted from one of the models outlined in this chapter.
Do you respond well to image?	Try a concept map approach. Just use key words and images to outline your thoughts.
Do you like to discuss things?	If you are happy to take a more open approach, think about a blog or setting up a discussion board. If you do this, remember that other people will have access to it so it is important to keep the information anonymous.

A reflective process does not allow us to take anything for granted. We need to be able to walk away from things in order to bring them into focus and the act of writing things on paper (or a screen) provides the distance we may need to do this.

The important thing is to start. Set aside 15 minutes and just write.

Reflecting with others

Sharing your reflections with others can be a very rewarding and enlightening process. By discussing your reflections, you will hear different perspectives and be able to benefit from others' experiences.

Figure 4.6 Reflecting with others

One informal strategy would be to set up a support group with some of your peers. This could be done using a form of social media or by meeting in person.

A more structured way of doing this might be through the use of peer observations. In this case you would arrange to observe your peers (and vice versa) and follow this with an objective discussion about the lesson. It is important in this instance that the focus is on your own learning and not on assessing your peers.

An alternative approach is the use of a more formal lesson study. This is a collaborative approach to professional learning originating from Japan. It is a methodical analysis of classroom teaching conducted collectively by a group of teachers. Typically, the cycle would involve a small group planning a chosen lesson. One person would teach while the others observe with a focus on a selection of case study learners. The lesson is then evaluated and revised and a second research lesson would be taught.

In practice it would look something like Figure 4.7.

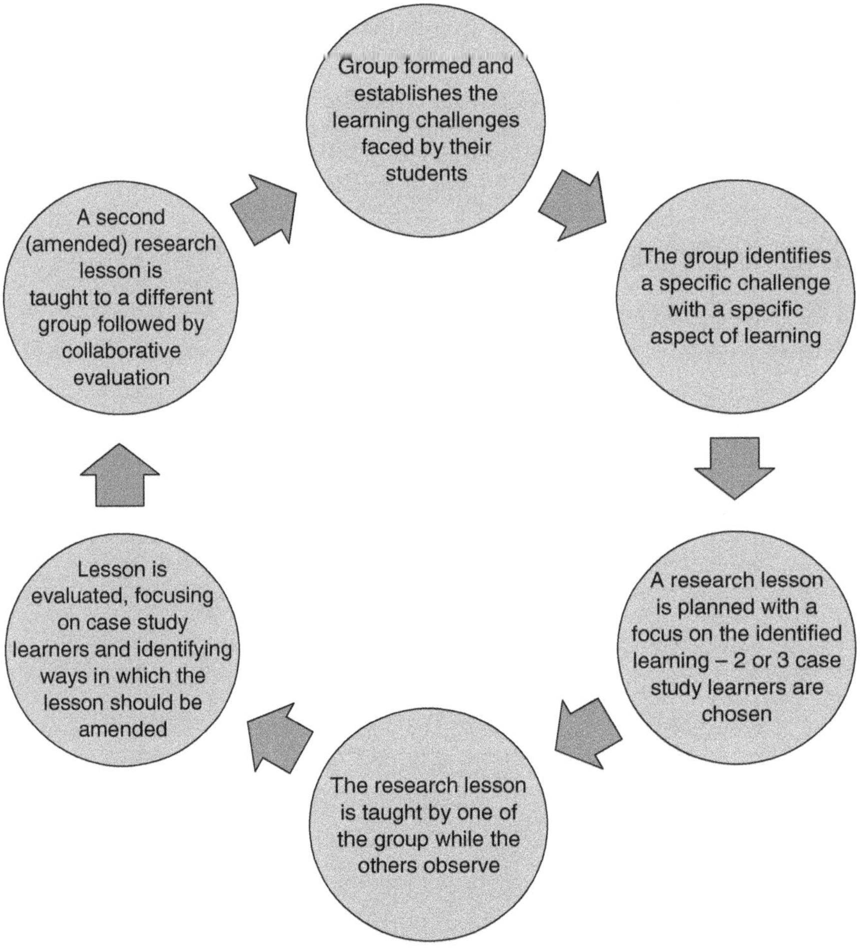

Figure 4.7 Lesson study

The darker side to reflection

It is difficult to imagine anything 'dark' about the process of reflection. If done well, this can be a very powerful tool which can be transformative. However, there are some potential pitfalls which should be mentioned.

When people are busy with the 'bread-and-butter' activities of their work it can be difficult to take the time to objectively reflect on professional practice and as a result the activity can become difficult. This may also be the case for trainees who are juggling several aspects of study while at the same time getting to grips with classroom teaching. As a result, the process of reflection can become mechanical and done to 'tick' the appropriate box rather than to critically evaluate teaching and learning.

The application of reflective practice to teaching also requires an understanding of professional ethics which relate to confidentiality and showing respect for others. While it is entirely appropriate to discuss your feelings about a particular event, specific reference to others should be avoided and it should be remembered that the focus is on improving *your* practice which does not involve making judgements on your colleagues.

It should also be acknowledged that the process of reflection can have an intense emotional impact on the person reflecting so does have the potential to be harmful. Brookfield refers to it as laying down psychological dynamite:

> *Questioning the assumptions on which we act and exploring alternative ideas are not only difficult but also psychologically explosive . . .*
>
> (Brookfield, 1990: 178)

The nature of reflection does lead us to strive for constant improvement and this contains the inherent danger of self-flagellation and a potentially negative frame of mind. Therefore it is imperative to remember the key principle of objectivity, noting that criticality (which in this context refers to purposeful thinking) does not necessarily mean criticising. It is also important to ensure that the process is contextualised with a clear purpose and does not simply become egocentric navel gazing.

A further danger is that reflection can be used to justify existing practice which potentially may mean reinforcing practice that is not effective. Where models of reflection are used in a routine or instrumental way the process can become self-justification without the application of critical analysis.

Things to think about

How important is reflective practice in understanding and developing your teaching? In what ways can it help you to develop your confidence in the classroom? What 'dangers' do you need to be aware of if you want this to become an instructive and potentially transformative process?

Now that you have an understanding of some popular models of reflection and approaches to recording reflective practice it should be much easier to think about the ways in which you could build this activity into your schedule.

In a nutshell

The following resource can be photocopied and used as a revision tool or a prompt for discussion with your peers. It is designed to get you to think about the many sources of feedback you can use to improve your practice.

Reflective journals

Reflective practice is the process of learning and developing through objective examination. In effect we are 'witnessing' our own experiences so that we can consider them in more detail. The key to this is learning how to take an objective perspective as if we are on the outside looking in. For anyone working in a professional context this is an important activity as the very nature of professionalism is embodied by a number of characteristics such as honesty, integrity and self-regulation.

One way to formalise the process of reflection is by keeping a reflective journal but *where do you start?* Key considerations for any reflective journal include honesty while recognising that the journal may be an assessed task; it is also a tool for personal and professional development and as such must be based on your own, honest evaluations. Ethical considerations should also be considered, particularly issues of confidentiality and anonymity. Finally, you need to think about the format for the journal.

Do you want to handwrite it? Would you prefer a free-flowing approach with limited structure? Would you like to share your journal through a particular medium?

Putting it into practice

- Create space in your week for journal writing. Set a date and time and make this a habit.
- Think about how and when you will use your journal to help you select an appropriate format.
- Adopt a 'healthy' approach to your journal by recognising the scope for development.
- Experiment with different approaches to find one that really works for you.
- Think about ways in which you can involve others such as your mentor or peers.

Source: Moon (2006).

Suggestions for further reading

Bolton, GEJ (2014) *Reflective Practice: Writing and Professional Development*, 4th edn. London: Sage.

Moon, JA (2006) *Learning Journals: A Handbook for Reflective Practice and Professional Development*, 2nd edn. Oxford: Routledge.

References

Brookfield, SD (1990) 'Using critical incidents to explore learners' assumptions', in J Mezirow (ed.), *Fostering Critical Reflection in Adulthood*. San Francisco: Jossey-Bass, pp. 177–93.

Brookfield, S (1995) *Becoming a Critically Reflective Teacher*. San-Francisco: Jossey-Bass.

Dewey, J (1933) *How We Think: A Restatement of the Relation of Reflective Thinking to the Educative Process*. New York: DC Heath.

Gibbs, G (1988) *Learning by Doing: A Guide to Teaching and Learning*. London: Longman.

Kirkpatrick, DL (1976) 'Evaluation of training', in RL Craig (ed.), *Training and Development Handbook: A Guide to Human Resource Development*. New York: McGraw-Hill.

Moon, JA (2006) *Learning Journals: A Handbook for Reflective Practice and Professional Development*, 2nd edn. Oxford: Routledge.

Schön, DA (1983) *The Reflective Practitioner: How Professionals Think in Action*. New York: Basic Books.

5

Using feedback for your own development

In this chapter we will explore:

- **how to get the most out of feedback;**
- **using lesson observations to develop your teaching;**
- **setting SMART targets.**

Introduction

As we discussed in the previous chapter, reflecting is a great way of improving your own professional practice. When cocooned in your own classroom or workshop, it is easy to lock out the outside world and assume that the way you do things is the one best way, but remember: 'Those who fail to learn from history are doomed to repeat it' (Santayana, 1905).

To continue to improve as a teacher it is important to make sure that you listen to those around you, in particular the people whose job it is to support your development, such as your tutors and mentor. While becoming a better teacher doesn't necessarily mean you adopt other people's ideas, it is useful to help you think about your teaching, taking into account what others say and then put into practice ideas that work for you.

As a professional teacher, you are also likely to be asked by others for advice and guidance, so it is important you have a good understanding of the role of feedback in professional development. Getting into the habit of reflecting, both in the classroom and after the session has finished, is good.

Figure 5.1 Ostrich

Reflection

The story of the black belt

Consider the story below and reflect on how this applies to your lessons:

A martial artist is kneeling before the master sensei in a ceremony to receive a hard-earnt black belt. After years of relentless training, the student has finally reached a pinnacle of achievement in the discipline.

'Before granting the belt, you must pass just one more test,' says the sensei.

'I am ready,' responds the student, expecting perhaps one final round of sparring.

'You must answer the essential question: "What is the true meaning of the black belt?"'

'It is the end of my journey,' says the student. 'A well-deserved reward for all my hard work.' The sensei waits for more. Clearly, he is not satisfied. Finally, the sensei speaks.

'You are not yet ready for the black belt. Return in one year.'

A year later, the student kneels again in front of the sensei. 'What is the true meaning of the black belt?' asks the sensei.

'A symbol of distinction and the highest achievement in what I do,' says the student. The sensei says nothing for many minutes, waiting. Clearly, he is still not satisfied. Finally, he speaks.

'You are still not ready for the black belt. Return in one year.'

A year later, the student kneels once again in front of the sensei. And for a final time the sensei asks: 'What is the true meaning of the black belt?'

(Continued)

'The black belt represents the beginning - the start of a never-ending journey of discipline, work and the pursuit of an ever-higher standard,' says the student.

The sensei smiles and answers: 'Yes. You are now ready to receive the black belt and begin your work.'

Adapted from Collins and Porras (1994).

The story is designed to get you to think about your course, and also your teaching. It is fine, and indeed very healthy, to congratulate yourself when things go well during a session but it is always important to keep learning and to keep striving to improve yourself as a professional. Your teaching certificate is a mere starting point.

The purpose of feedback

Figure 5.2 Feedback loop

The purpose of feedback is to provide information and comment on what has occurred in the past. Within education, this is generally linked to the goal of improving things for the future. It is likely that you have come to the conclusion that teaching is more of an art than a science in that there are often very few guaranteed answers. Teaching the exact same session, in exactly the same way but on a different day sometimes leads to a completely different outcome. This can be frustrating and it is why feedback is so important. By using it we can assess, modify and hopefully improve our teaching.

Feedback and feedforward?

In education, we use two approaches to improving our own and others' development. The first approach looks at the past and makes judgements on what has gone before. This is known as feed*back*. Feedback is fundamental in building strong foundations for our development; ignoring it means we are likely to make the same mistakes again and again. Think about the parable of the man who built his house on sand. When the rains came down and the winds blew, it fell. Instead of listening to the feedback, reflecting on what he has learnt and changing, he merely repeated the same mistake, with the same consequence.

Figure 5.3 Sandcastle

Activity

Think about the difference between the following quotes:

'You're doing it all wrong!'

'Have you thought about reversing the order of the first two tasks?'

What are the differences in the way the feedback has been structured?

The first can be described as *judgemental* – it reports back on something you have done. The second is *developmental* – it is suggesting an alternative.

The second approach is known as feed*forward*. This builds on what has happened in the past and seeks to give advice for the future. Again, this is vital as it allows you to reflect on what you have done but, most importantly, it encourages you to continually seek to improve and to learn from the past.

In many ways, this reflects the approach that you take with your own students but it is also important to remember that by receiving both feedback and feedforward you can also improve your own practice.

Tips for making the most of feedback

It is much easier to learn from any mistakes when it is a two-way conversation – this is also true when receiving feedback and feedforward. Put yourself in the shoes of your students. If you advise them about how to improve their work, you would want to know that, if they don't understand what you have written, then they would be able to come and see you to ask for clarification. This is also true for advice on your professional practice. You need to be able to discuss things with fellow professionals with the overall aim of improving your professional practice.

Figure 5.4 Professional discussion

This is known as a professional discussion and will involve analysis of your practice. It is important that this is a two-way, open, meaningful dialogue rather than a one-way conversation where one person talks and the other listens passively.

So, when receiving feedback and feedforward think about the following.

1. **Regard all feedback as valuable.** Whether feedback is in the form of praise or criticism, you will get a lot more out of it if you value it.
2. **Feedback from anyone is useful.** While it is understandable to regard the feedback you get from mentors and tutors as authoritative, you can also get feedback all the time from fellow students and other people around you.
3. **Do not shrug off positive feedback.** When you are complimented on your work, there is a temptation to try to ease any feeling of embarrassment by saying, *'Well, it's not so special really.'*

It is healthy to accept praise and take a pride in your work. This helps you to accept the positive feedback, to build upon it and do even better next time.

4. **Practise thanking people for their positive feedback.** Simply saying, *'Thanks, I'm glad you liked that'* can be enough sometimes. When people are thanked for giving you praise or compliments, they are more likely to do so again, and this means more and better feedback for you.

5. **Do not get defensive when feedback is critical.** It is perfectly natural to try to protect yourself from the impact of criticism but remember this is also valuable as it provides you with information about potential development points.

6. **Thank people for critical feedback too.** Even though you might not exactly feel pleased. It can be useful to say something along the lines, *'Thanks for telling me about this, it will be useful for me in future.'*

7. **Do not just wait for feedback, ask for it!** Do not lose any opportunities to press gently for even more feedback. Ask questions, such as *'What do you think was the best thing I did here?'* and *'What would have been the most useful change I should make next time I do something similar?'*, and so on.

8. **For your academic work, look back at the feedback you have received so far.** You can often polish up an assignment quite quickly and avoid some of the things which caused you to lose marks last time.

9. **If you believe the group has the maturity for this approach, get the students to feed back on the lesson.** This can be very valuable with the right group. Something as simple as asking them to complete a sticky note at the end of the session can provide you with useful insight into the perspective of those sitting in your class.

Surviving and thriving on lesson observations

Being observed will always be a stressful time but you can make it less stressful by ensuring that there is a clear focus to any observation where at all possible. Different schools and colleges operate in different ways but in general there are three main approaches to observations:

1. Pre-planned observations are either judgemental or developmental in nature. These will occur at a specific time/date and might be either graded or ungraded.

2. 'Surprise' observations attempt to mimic the Ofsted approach. You will often be told the week that they will occur in but not the actual lesson. These observations are generally judgemental in nature.

3. 'Learning walks' consist of someone spending a short period of time (often 10–15 minutes) in a number of classrooms with a pre-arranged focus. Feedback will be given across all participants and, in general, the purpose of these observations is to develop a specific teaching area.

It is very easy to get defensive about all three types of observations but when done properly they can be a worthwhile source of information about how you can improve your teaching.

Observation checklist

Figure 5.5 Checklist

- **Where possible talk to the observer beforehand and agree a focus.** Select something where you know you can improve. Although it is nice to receive positive feedback about things that you know are already good, it will not help you to improve as a teacher.
- **Plan . . . but don't over-plan.** It is important to know what you are doing but it is also important to be flexible enough to change things during the lesson if there is a better way of doing things.
- **Organise the basics before the lesson.** This means making sure your photocopying is ready, you have a supply of pens and paper and that your register is with your lesson plan.
- **Have a plan in case technology fails.** There is a certain amount of inevitability in the fact that the computer always lets you down when you most need it. Make sure you have a 'plan B' if technology is not available.
- **Support staff.** If you have any assistants in the class with you then make sure that you have fully briefed them before the class.
- **Is your paperwork up to date?** The observer is likely to spend a fair amount of time looking through paperwork so make sure that any targets are current, class profiles are up to date and any additional needs have been noted.
- **Behaviour management strategies.** Having someone else in the room always affects how children behave so be prepared for changes in behaviour and have strategies to deal with it.

And finally remember – they will always find something! So don't get defensive when developmental points are raised. Discuss them, reflect on them and see what you can learn from them!

Using feedback to set SMART targets

Of course, the greatest feedback and feedforward in the world is useless if you don't act upon it. This is where SMART targets can be useful.

SMART stands for:

> **S**pecific
>
> **M**easurable
>
> **A**chievable
>
> **R**ealistic
>
> **T**ime Bounded

A good idea after every observation is to give yourself a few SMART targets that you can work on for your next lesson. An example might be:

> *'For my next Year 10 English class, I will ensure that I will set up a late desk and will make sure that anyone who is not on time is required to sit there.'*

This target is specific (it is in the Year 10 English class), measurable (we can see if latecomers are directed to this desk), achievable (this technique is common in schools), realistic (it is a good strategy to deal with latecomers) and time bounded (it will be put in place for the next lesson).

Activity

Ask a colleague to come into one of your next classes. The ideal class is one which you are comfortable with but maybe want to change approach or try something new. Before the lesson talk to your colleague and agree on a focus (this might be classroom management, stretching the most able or maybe starting the class). Ask them to concentrate on that aspect in their observation.

After the class hold a professional discussion and use your colleague's thoughts as an opportunity to reflect on your teaching. At the end of the discussion record two SMART targets for your next session with the group.

Creating SMART targets does require a little bit of practice but it is a very useful way to ensure you make the most out of feedback.

Things to think about

Being a professional involves constantly improving your practice and listening to the people around you. So, think about the people who can help your professional development – Who can you ask to help you improve? Could you use peer observation to support your reflective activities and develop specific targets? Remember that we can always improve and effective use of feedback is essential in this process.

In a nutshell

This resource can be photocopied and used as a revision tool or a prompt for discussion with your peers. It is designed to get you to think about the many sources of feedback you can use to improve your practice.

Feedback and feedforward

Obtaining feedback and feedforward is vital in ensuring that you improve your own professional practice. A professional discussion or two-way conversation can be used to stimulate ideas and to ensure that you continuously reflect and improve on your teaching.

A key point is to make sure that you use the discussion to improve your professional practice as sometimes it is easy to forget to apply the lessons learnt. Finally, remember that feedback is not a personal reflection on you, it is a reflection on the lesson.

Source: Capel *et al*. (2009).

A 360 degree observation

It is important to get feedback from as many sources as possible in order to set yourself targets, so try the following for one of your classes and see if the feedback is the same from everyone.

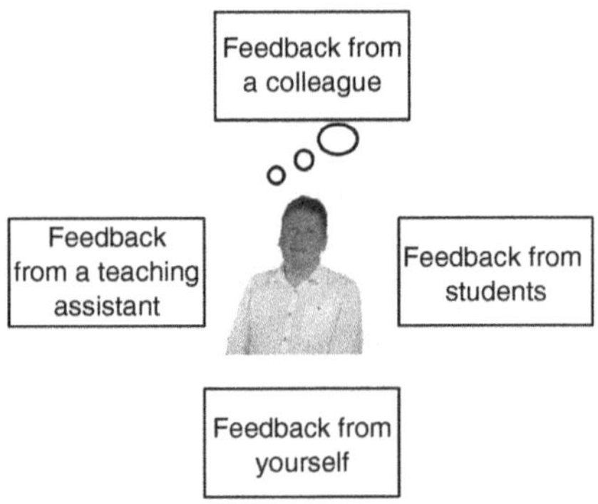

Suggestions for further reading

Moon, J (1999) *Reflection in Learning and Professional Development*. Abingdon: RoutledgeFalmer.

Zeichner, K and Liston, D (2014) *Reflective Teaching: An Introduction*, 2nd edn. Abingdon: RoutledgeFalmer.

References

Capel, S, Leask, M and Turner, T (2009) *Learning to Teach in the Secondary School*, 5th edn. Abingdon: Routledge.

Collins, J and Porras, J (1994) *Built to Last: Successful Habits of Visionary Companies*. New York: Harper Business.

Santayana, G (1905) *The Life of Reason: The Phases of Human Progress*. Alexandria: Library of Alexandria.

6

Potential barriers to teaching

In this chapter, we will explore:

- **the barriers that you might face when teaching a group;**
- **the difference between intrinsic and extrinsic barriers;**
- **how to overcome these barriers.**

Introduction

As a teacher, it is likely that you will feel under pressure to 'be your best' at all times. There is an expectation that we will spring into action as soon as we cross the threshold of our classroom, leaving all problems at the door. Sadly, while this is an aspiration, it is unrealistic for it to be an expectation. We all have days when things seem to go swimmingly, and others when, for whatever reason, they just don't. The important thing is to acknowledge this and to recognise potential causes so that we can mitigate the impact wherever possible.

Potential barriers to teaching

Barriers can be put into two groups: first, intrinsic barriers (those centred on the teacher) and, second, extrinsic (those centred elsewhere). Once we have identified a particular barrier we can start working on a solution.

Although some barriers are obvious – such as managing your time in order to prepare sufficiently for teaching – others are less obvious. Inevitably this makes finding a solution more of a challenge; for example, if you are consistently struggling to engage a particular class, it is often tricky to understand whether it is something that you are doing that is causing the problem or whether the problem lies elsewhere.

Intrinsic barriers tend to be linked to either your previous experiences or, as outlined in Chapter 1, to engrained values, attitudes and beliefs, which in turn inform behaviours and habits. In many cases

Figure 6.1 Brick wall

these are so deeply held that we are not always aware that we have them, which makes them very difficult to change. Only by confronting them can we learn to behave or react in a different way.

Extrinsic barriers are likely to be more noticeable which, on the surface, makes them more straightforward to deal with. However, the fact that they are in the conscious rather than unconscious part of your brain means that they can become a source of immense frustration as you are able to see the problem but the solution is sometimes difficult to grasp.

Managing intrinsic barriers

Managing intrinsic barriers to teaching involves turning our attention inwards and looking at ourselves. We all have our individual ways of looking at the world and this influences our reaction to certain events and how we perceive things. The activity below is designed to get you to think about how we live so much of our life on autopilot, leading to automatic thoughts, actions and behaviours. While this in itself is not a problem, it can become a barrier if we fail to understand how our engrained behaviours influence everyday life.

Activity

Imagine that you are driving your car and want to put it into reverse gear. Sitting perfectly still and with no movement of your hands, explain either to a friend or just by talking out loud, how you would do this.

For those of you who don't drive, think about another action that involves a kinaesthetic activity such as typing your name, then explain it without using your hands.

Frames of reference

Figure 6.2 Frames of reference

Most people find this activity difficult as the actions have become second nature and we no longer have to think about them. We might call them patterns of behaviour, routines or learnt behaviour.

What the activity shows is that there are very clear patterns of behaviour in our lives. While this is not necessarily a problem in something straightforward like putting a car into reverse gear, in other situations, these learnt behaviours can act as a barrier. This is often the case when it refers to thoughts and actions. These engrained behaviours are termed 'frames of reference'. Just as we learn how to put our car into reverse gear, we also tend to learn behaviours and approaches which manifest themselves in how we react to things. These frames of reference are imprinted on our brain and are generally so deep that we often do not even realise we have them until we analyse them.

Figure 6.3 Engrained behaviours

Just as we have our own frames of reference, so do our students. These have often been set some time ago and can be difficult to change. They may be based on learning through experiences or through formal and informal learning situations and refer to repeated patterns where perceptions, beliefs, behaviours and sometimes even the things we say are executed with an almost parrot-like automaticity.

In some cases, our frames of reference may be viewed as positive – for example, you may be someone who sees criticism as feedback which helps you to improve what you do. In this way, your response to criticism will be to value it as something you can reflect on and utilise to improve your practice. Alternatively, you may view criticism as a personal insult, in which case the way you respond to it is more likely to be emotional rather than rational.

According to Mezirow (1997) our frames of reference can only be changed, or *transformed*, by analysis of them. In a sense, when we do this we are reframing our thoughts about particular experiences and in doing so are able to achieve a different perspective which in turn may lead to different behaviours.

Reflection

Think about one routine that you have in your day-to-day life. This might be connected to your teaching or it could be something that relates to another aspect of your life. Try to think why you complete the routine in the way you do. Is there any logic to how you do it or are there alternative approaches? Try to understand your reasons for doing what you do. Once you have understood your routine, think how you could do this differently.

Presuppositions

The habitual ways in which we learn to think about things may also be influenced by our presuppositions. If we presuppose something, we are making an assumption about it, so a presupposition could be described as an assumption we have about the world which is presented as a 'taken for granted' truth. We may, for example, presuppose the following.

- People are good.
- Not all people are good.
- The world is a safe place.
- The world is a scary place.
- You can trust most people.
- You can trust people you know well.
- If we work hard we will achieve the things we want.
- Achievement is down to luck not hard work.

Any of the above beliefs may or may not be true. We may have had some experience in the past which proves the 'truth' in any one of those statements, we may have been told these things by influential others. Either way, if any of these are presuppositions we hold true they will influence the way we approach and experience the events of our lives which in turn will influence how we react to others and ourselves.

Neuro-linguistic programming (NLP) was developed in the 1970s by Richard Bandler and John Grinder, who saw the opportunities in combining thinking from a number of disciplines (in this case, linguistics, systems thinking and psychotherapy) to create a model of interpersonal communication concerned with successful patterns of behaviour and the subjective experiences surrounding them. Although it has been subject to criticism because it is not considered a 'pure science', there are many aspects of NLP which are useful in helping us to understand our behaviours and the potential for change. One aspect which is useful in a teaching and learning context is the way in which presuppositions are employed as a basis for reflection. The following activity includes some common presuppositions from NLP for you to consider in relation to your professional practice.

Activity

Think about the following ten presuppositions taken from NLP and consider how they are similar or different to your current beliefs.

- The map is not the territory.
- The meaning of a communication is the response you get.
- You cannot not communicate.

(Continued)

- Every behaviour has a positive intention.
- People make the best choices available to them.
- There is no such thing as failure only feedback.
- If what you are doing isn't working, do something else.
- We have all the resources within us to achieve what we want.
- Choice is better than no choice.
- Everyone lives in their unique model of the world.

What is your interpretation of each of the statements? How do these relate to your own presuppositions? Could the statements be used to challenge your current thinking?

If you take this a step further and consider how one or more of these statements may relate to teaching and learning, your reflections may be a useful entry for your reflective log.

The imposter syndrome

Figure 6.4 The imposter syndrome

A common feeling among teachers, no matter how experienced they are, is that at some point they will be exposed as a fraud and that their students and colleagues will eventually realise that they haven't got all the answers. Clance and Imes (1978) called this feeling 'the imposter syndrome'; when left unchecked it can become a persistent barrier to teaching as it leads to a lack of confidence, an unwillingness to try something different and, in more extreme cases, feelings of dread when confronted by a class.

Teaching relies a lot on confidence and if you feel like an imposter then this can have a significant impact; you begin to doubt what you are saying and once you start portraying an uncertain or nervous persona in front of a class, students are often quick to take advantage.

There are a number of things you can do to conquer this barrier but most importantly please realise that you are not alone! As mentioned, almost every single teacher you meet will have faced this barrier before and will know how you are feeling. Many staffrooms operate under 'Fight Club Rules'. This relates to the scene in the film *Fight Club* (1999) where Tyler Durden explains that the first rule of Fight Club is you do not talk about Fight Club. In a nutshell, it means that what is talked about in the staffroom, stays in the staffroom and hence this creates a safe haven for teachers. This means that you can express how you feel without fear of being judged. If this does not work then there are five things that you can do which might help you:

- **Celebrate success.** It is very easy to focus on everything that goes wrong in the classroom but it is important to make sure that you recognise your successes. A good idea is to make sure that you keep any celebratory emails, letters or cards that you receive from people. When you are struggling then re-read the words and hopefully your confidence will return.
- **Stop comparing yourself to others.** This is a classic mistake that teachers make. We are all individuals and to compare yourself to another teacher is often counterproductive. While it is fine to identify positive features in other teachers that you can use in your own teaching, remember that merely copying someone else is likely to lead to problems as what works for them is not always appropriate for you.
- **Acknowledge the imposter syndrome.** By acknowledging the issue, you can start dealing with it. Keep reminding yourself that the vast majority of teachers will have felt exactly the same way as you and they have battled through it!
- **Embrace the imperfection.** There is a tendency as a new teacher to expect everything to go to plan. We look at our lesson plans and for many of us there will be worry or panic if things veer from what we envisaged. This is a normal feeling but, in reality, the lesson plan represents a prediction. Accept that things will not always go as you envisaged and remember that this is not always a bad thing.
- **Faking it doesn't work.** To some extent we are constantly 'acting' as teachers – there is an expectation that even if we are not feeling our best, that we carry on regardless. While this is often necessary in a classroom, always acknowledge to yourself how you feel. As ever with the imposter syndrome, it is important to recognise how you feel and this will be the first step towards dealing with it.

Extrinsic barriers

Orr and Simmons (2010) discussed the problems many trainee teachers have in making sure that they balance the role of teacher with the role of student, a status referred to as 'dual identity'. Not only does the extra pressure of studying for your teacher training qualification impact on the time you have available to complete your teaching duties but also the differing roles require separate skills which can challenge you. In addition, you are an expert in your subject so there will be pressure on you to maintain your expertise in the subject as well. This all adds to the pressures on you, as well as adding to your workload.

Activity

Imagine that you have just got home from a heavy teaching day. It is a Thursday evening and as you glance at your list of things to do, it has the following things on it:

- Complete PGCE assignment for tomorrow (you estimate you have about another two hours' work on this)
- Finish preparing your Year 10 class for 9am tomorrow (about one hour)
- Mark 20 essays that you promised the class that you would do for tomorrow
- Go for a celebration drink with your best friend as he/she has got a new job
- Make sure you post a present to your sister for her birthday
- Make sure that you complete a safeguarding report regarding an incident a student told you about as you were leaving school
- Have dinner

The time is now 6pm. Look at the tasks on your list and formulate a plan for the evening.

The reality is that there is no easy way of balancing the various demands but this is an essential skill to have as a teacher. A lack of time is a key extrinsic barrier to tackle and failure to manage your time effectively will lead to you having to do everything at the last minute and potentially not prioritising correctly.

Looking at the list given there are a few things that could be viewed as critical. The safeguarding issue is of vital importance and making sure that you are prepared for tomorrow is also very important. At the other end of the scale, while it is important to maintain a social life as a teacher, celebrations can often be fitted in around other events.

Having strategies to deal with your workload is crucial. We have already talked about the urgency grid (see Chapter 2) but other strategies can be brought in. If you know that you are going to have a busy week then prepare meals in advance, so that you can heat them up rather than make them from scratch. Schedule time for assignments in advance rather than waiting for the due date to arrive and manage the expectations of your classes when it comes to marking. Don't promise them something that you can't deliver!

The importance of preparation

Most of the other extrinsic barriers to teaching become apparent when you step into your classroom. It is very easy to see teaching as something that exists in a vacuum but the reality is that if you do not prepare properly for the lesson, you run the risk of meeting barriers which could have been removed with appropriate preparation. Getting to the room early and doing a ten-point check can ensure that barriers are removed from the start:

1. Is the room set up in a way that reflects your lesson plan (e.g. if you are doing groupwork can students cluster together?)
2. Are you going to be using a seating plan? If so, is it easily available?
3. Are there any areas of the classroom that are hidden? If so, how are you going to manage them?
4. Have you got enough chairs?
5. Are all your resources easily accessible?
6. Are there any distractions in the classroom, e.g. resources left from previous classes?
7. Are there any distractions outside the classroom? If so, would you be better to pull the blinds down?
8. Have you decided what to do about latecomers to ensure that they cause minimal disruption to everybody?
9. Have you briefed your teaching assistant about today's lesson?
10. Have you reminded yourself about what you are looking to get out of the class?

Figure 6.5 The goldfish

Going through the ten-point checklist does not guarantee a perfect class but what it does do is give you the chance to think about potential extrinsic barriers to teaching. So, for example, if you are timetabled in a science lab where there are fixed benches yet are planning on doing groupwork then you can think about how you are going to change things around before students arrive. Again, your solution might not completely solve the problem but it means you are prepared to overcome these barriers and you will come across as in control and organised. Although we are always searching for the 'perfect' lesson, remember, in the words of Vince Lombardi, *Perfection is not attainable, but if we chase perfection we can catch excellence.*

Things to think about

It is a fact of teaching life that there are often barriers to the successful implementation of your plans for the lesson. Even on days when things are going exactly to plan, you know that at some point you will have to overcome an obstacle. An important thing to think about is why those barriers exist and how we overcome them. The intrinsic barriers discussed in this chapter are common to many people and it is important to recognise them – once we understand their existence, they become much easier to deal with, so why not think about your own personal barriers and what you can do to negotiate them?

In a nutshell

This resource can be photocopied and used as a revision tool or a prompt for discussion with your peers. It relates to the concept of a frame of reference which was discussed earlier in the chapter.

Frames of reference

A frame of reference refers to the way in which you view things. This will be a complex set of assumptions, attitudes and perceptions which help frame our reality (Tversky and Kahneman, 1981).

These frames are generally so engrained in us that we are not aware that they are there until we are confronted with them. Only then can we change them, or in the words of Mezirow (1997), we can be transformed.

Constant analysis of our frames of reference helps to stop us stagnating and ensures that we do not fall into patterns of behaviour which are not always positive.

Source: Mezirow (1997).

Putting it into practice

Reflection is one of the key ways of changing the frames of references of yourself and others. One exercise you can do is to get your students to identify a lesson where they felt disengaged and get them to concept map the reasons why. This way they can identify any barriers and you can work on solutions.

While they do the exercise, you do the same thing.

When the exercise is finished review it in a week's time to see if the solutions have been used.

What else could you do?

7

The resilient teacher

In this chapter we will explore:

- **what emotional resilience looks like;**
- **ways of building emotional resilience;**
- **approaches to minimising stress.**

Introduction

For most people there will be times when it is necessary to find strategies to cope with the requirements of working life, whatever the job level or work context. Teaching is a role which has many emotional demands and has been recognised as one of the most challenging occupations in terms of experiences of work-related anxiety and stress (Health and Safety Executive, 2016). For trainee teachers these demands may be increased as a result of the dual roles undertaken as both teacher and student. This can mean you have twice the demands, so it is important to develop strategies to build your own resilience.

What does the resilient teacher look like?

Resilience refers to our ability to develop positive strategies to manage workload, create a work-life balance and adopt approaches to cope with events which are challenging. Emotional resilience could be described as the way we recover from events or an ability to 'bounce back' from adversity and is an essential skill for any role which presents a range of regular challenges. So what does emotional resilience looks like?

Suggestions for further reading

Tversky, A and Kahneman, D (1974) 'Judgments under uncertainty', *Science*, 185 (4157): 1124–31.

References

Bavister, S and Vickers, A (2010) *Essential NLP*. Oxford: Hodder Education.

Clance, P and Imes, S (1978) 'The imposter phenomenon in high achieving women: dynamics and therapeutic intervention', *Psychotherapy Theory, Research and Practice,* 15 (3): 1–8.

Mezirow, J (1997) *Transformative Dimensions of Adult Learning*. San Francisco: Jossey-Bass.

Orr, K and Simmons, R (2010) 'Dual identities: the in-service trainee experience in the English further education sector', *Journal of Vocational Education and Training,* 62 (1): 75–88.

Tversky, A and Kahneman, D (1981) 'The framing of decisions and psychology of choice', *Science,* 211: 453–8.

Figure 7.1 The resilient teacher

Reflection

Imagine you have just been given a very difficult assignment that you need to pass in order to progress on your course. You have already done some reading but still don't understand the topic enough to write about it. Your peers don't seem to be struggling with the assignment and you are beginning to question why you are finding it so difficult. What do you do?

Is your immediate response to tell yourself you will rise to the challenge, or do you doubt your abilities and begin to slump into despair? If it is the former then congratulations on your strong self-belief and, if the latter, don't worry – the skills you need to overcome this hurdle can be learnt.

Emotional resilience includes things like self-awareness, the ability to be reflective, a sense of humour and optimism, and, though it seems that these might simply be personality traits, there is evidence to suggest they are skills we can all develop. As they are important skills for teachers we will be exploring many of them in other chapters. In this chapter the focus will be on the three key pillars of emotional resilience.

Self-efficacy

Self-efficacy can be defined as a person's beliefs about their capability to exercise influence over events which affect their lives. The term was developed by Albert Bandura (1977) as part of social cognitive theory which acknowledges the role of cognition and motivation in directing our

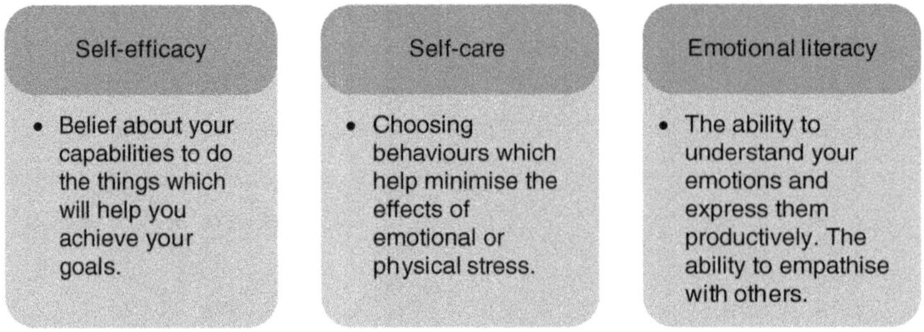

Figure 7.2 The pillars of emotional resilience

behaviours. According to Bandura, what people think, believe and feel affects how they behave and has an impact on how we motivate ourselves to achieve desired outcomes.

Bandura referred to self-efficacy as part of the 'self-system' which has a significant influence in how we perceive and respond to a range of situations as well as our ability to direct action which helps us to achieve the outcomes we want. All individuals can identify things they want to change but how they approach these challenges will differ. Individuals with a strong sense of self-efficacy tend to view challenges as problems to be mastered, whereas those with a weak sense of self-efficacy will believe that these things are beyond their capabilities and as a result may avoid difficult tasks. For example, a person with a strong sense of self-efficacy may:

- see problems as challenges;
- develop an intrinsic interest in activities;
- form a stronger sense of commitment to their interests and activities;
- recover quickly from setbacks and disappointments;
- sustain efforts in the face of failure.

On the other hand, someone with a weaker sense of self-efficacy may:

- avoid challenging tasks;
- have lower aspirations;
- have less commitment to goals;
- believe that difficult tasks and situations are beyond their capabilities;
- focus on personal failings and negative outcomes;
- lose confidence in personal abilities.

Self-efficacy is developed through experiences, emotions, imagination and observing others. The term 'mastery experiences' is used to describe self-efficacy based on enjoying success through mastering a skill or technique leading to an increased belief in our ability to achieve desired outcomes. If this is the case, the resilient teacher would be persistent in finding ways to overcome obstacles through effort and perseverance. Another influential form of experience is that described as 'vicarious experience' which relates to our observation of others. Seeing people we perceive as similar to ourselves achieve success through their efforts is likely to raise our own beliefs in this possibility.

Bandura also believed that we are influenced by 'verbal persuasion' from significant people in our lives (such as parents, teachers and managers) and these experiences can strengthen or weaken our beliefs in our ability to succeed. Based on these two points, the resilient teacher would observe and model the behaviours of other successful teachers and recognise the importance of feedback offered by the people who can provide support.

The importance of 'imaginal experience' is widely recognised in other fields such as sports and coaching. This refers to our ability to imagine the behaviours we want to exhibit by visualising what we want to achieve. Although this may seem like an unrealistic approach, the simple act of imagining an event allows us the opportunity to practise it in our minds and this in itself is a useful activity.

A final consideration is our emotional state. High levels of stress or anxiety can make us feel more vulnerable whereas experience of positive emotions can boost our confidence.

It is important to remember that we are not born with a level of self-efficacy that we maintain throughout our lives. Developing a strong sense of self-efficacy is something we can enhance with practice and the resilient teacher is the one who learns how to do this. Think of it as a continuum where you might start with a weak sense of self-efficacy but, through learning different ways of thinking and approaching tasks, you move through the continuum until you achieve the outcome you want.

Figure 7.3 The continuum of self-efficacy

Activity

Think of something that really challenges your self-efficacy, for example public speaking or maybe a job interview. Write down a list of things you could do to help build your self-efficacy in relation to this challenge.

Self-care

In simplistic terms, self-care could just mean looking after ourselves. At a very basic level this includes things such as personal hygiene, ensuring we eat healthily and dress appropriately and so on. Some people may even equate self-care with more indulgent activities, such as going on holiday or having beauty treatments. Our description will be based on the assumption that you already know how to take care of the basic things and will focus on those things which will make a difference to your experience of being both a teacher and a student.

Self-care means choosing behaviours which are supportive and balance the effects of emotional or physical stress. It includes eating healthily, exercising and getting enough sleep and it is recommended that you ensure time is built into your daily routines to ensure these things happen. It also means managing your emotions in healthy ways which meet your personal needs.

Activity

The following list includes a number of strategies for coping with difficult times. Think about the list and rate the activities from 1 to 10 (1 being 'this doesn't/wouldn't work at all for me' and 10 being 'this works/could work really well for me').

Taking a tea/coffee break

Doing a few yoga poses

Taking a walk in the fresh air

Doing a challenging physical exercise like running

Reading something you are interested in

Sharing ideas, thoughts with others

Singing

Drawing

Meditating

The list is not intended to be a guide – the real object of that exercise is to get you thinking about what works for you. Any other activity which gets you off the treadmill for a short period of time will do the trick.

Emotional literacy

Emotional literacy refers to our ability to express our feelings by acknowledging and naming emotions as well as our capacity to listen to and empathise with others; this is closely linked to the concept of emotional intelligence. According to Goleman emotional intelligence refers to *Being able to rein in emotional impulse; to read another's innermost feelings; to handle relationships smoothly* (Goleman, 1996: xiii). Developing these skills has the potential to improve communication, empathy and relationships, skills which are essential for professionals whose roles involve day-to-day contact with a diverse range of individuals.

Figure 7.4 The hamster wheel

There are four key elements to emotional intelligence:

- **Self-awareness** – knowing what we are feeling and understanding the impact this may have on others.
- **Self-regulation** – being able to direct emotions in a way that anticipates consequences (avoiding acting on impulse).
- **Motivation** – using emotions to achieve goals, enjoy learning and persevere in the face of obstacles.
- **Empathy** – understanding and sensing the feelings of others.
- **Social skills** – managing relationships and prompting desired responses from others.

It is likely that you will face a number of challenges during your training and it is very important that you develop some strategies to help you deal with those challenges in productive ways. Think about the events which have the potential to cause you anxiety, for example passing assessments or being observed on your teaching, and try to anticipate the ways in which you can manage these events so that you achieve the most successful outcome. This might mean practical preparation, such as ensuring you read relevant literature and prepare thoroughly for teaching, but it can also mean managing your emotional state to ensure that events are not hijacked by unexpected emotional responses.

Adopting this approach will help you to feel in control of things which in turn will reduce any anxiety you might be experiencing. However, there may be some things that you struggle to let go of; if that is the case, try working through the 'worry decision tree' as a way of calming yourself. This is a simple technique which is helpful in focusing energy on the things we can do something about.

The technique involves writing down whatever is worrying you then answering the following questions:

> Is there anything I can do about this?
>
> If the answer is 'yes', work out what to do or how to find out what to do and make a list.
>
> If the answer is 'no', stop worrying and distract yourself.
>
> Next, ask yourself if there is anything you can do right now.

If the answer is 'yes' then write down what you could do and do it now. Then stop worrying and distract yourself.

If the answer is 'no', plan what you could do and when. Then stop worrying and distract yourself.

Adapter from Butler and Hope (2007)

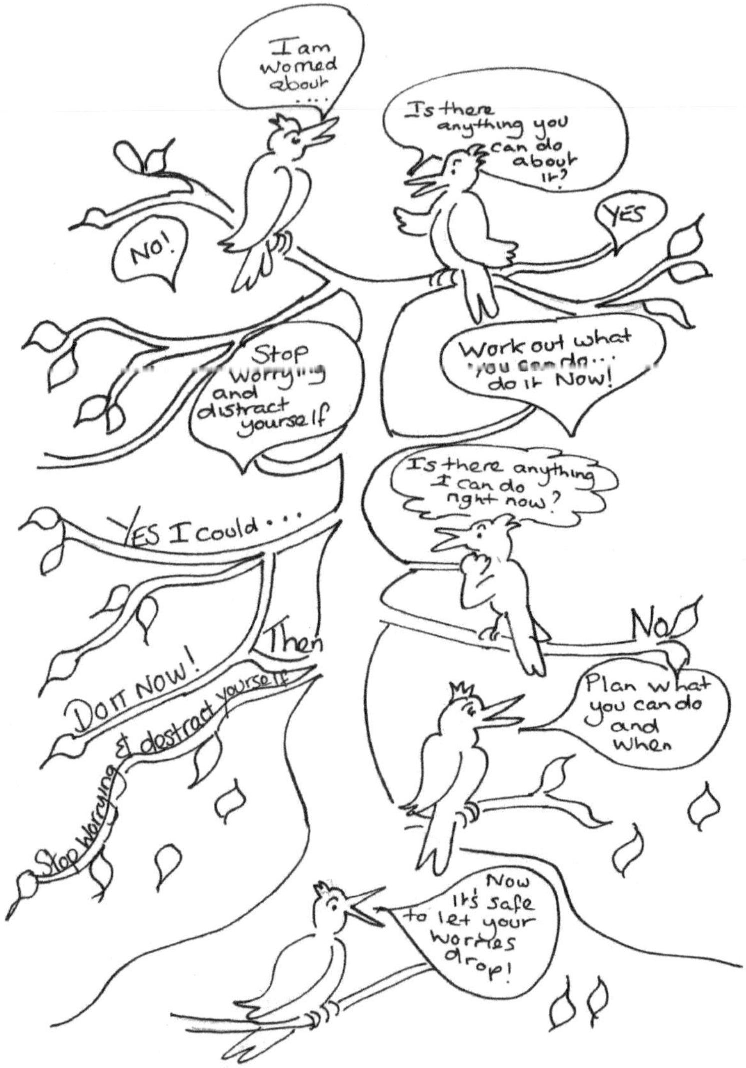

Figure 7.5 The worry decision tree

Managing stress

The resilient teacher is able to manage their workload in ways which allow time to do things outside of work and thereby manage overall stress. While it can be very tempting to spend all of your waking hours on ensuring you are on top of things, this approach is not sustainable and ultimately will make you less effective in your role. In Chapter 2 we introduced you to some strategies you could use to manage your time effectively and would recommend that you select some of those strategies to try to find approaches that work for you.

According to the Health and Safety Executive (2016) over 11 million work days were lost due to stress and this accounted for 45 per cent of working days lost due to ill health. These statistics also highlight that stress was more prevalent in public service industries including education. This might paint a somewhat depressing picture but it is important to remember that you have some control over your response to stress and if you have an awareness of coping strategies from the outset you are much more likely to overcome any hurdles which present themselves.

Your feelings are important

It is very easy to fall into the trap of taking care of others and neglecting ourselves. This approach is prevalent in working environments where the welfare of others is a priority. Your fundamental values in relation to teaching are very likely to include caring for your students, being aware of their well-being and ensuring that you support their development. These are sound principles on which to base your practice, so long as you remember that you also need to apply them to yourself. It is very important that we manage our own well-being as, without this, we are unable to do the same for others. You are not a robot, you too have emotions which will affect your responses to situations differently on different days and while you may think that this is something you just have to hide so that you can get on with your job, it is worth remembering that, however good your acting skills, some of what you are thinking and feeling will impact on the classroom environment. There is a popular quote by Ginott which illustrates this eloquently:

> *I've come to a frightening conclusion that I am the decisive element in the classroom. It's my personal approach that creates the climate. It's my daily mood that makes the weather. As a teacher, I possess a tremendous power to make a child's life miserable or joyous. I can be a tool of torture or an instrument of inspiration. I can humiliate or heal. In all situations, it is my response that decides whether a crisis will be escalated or de-escalated and a child humanized or dehumanized.*
>
> (Ginott, 1972: 15, 16)

Reflection

Take a moment and think about all the feelings you had yesterday - what do you notice? Name the emotions you felt and think about how they influenced your behaviour. This might be a useful thing to record in your reflective journal.

Because you are interacting with different people all day long, a key part of teaching is learning how to manage relationships. To do this you do need to acknowledge how you are feeling and work out what strategies help you in situations you find difficult. Keeping a reflective log is useful here as it will help you to establish patterns. Remember to log how you felt about particular interactions, what behaviour those feelings prompted and then how you felt about your own behaviour. There are some strategies you can implement to help you cope in more difficult situations – the reading at the end of this chapter will be helpful for that. Some initial things to try are:

- **Breathing.** This does sound obvious but calming your breathing really does help calm your mood. Try the simple 7-11 technique: breathe in through the nose to the count of seven and breathe out of the mouth to the count of 11. It takes some practice but when you have the technique you will notice an impact.
- **Pausing.** Don't always respond to things immediately. If something has provoked an unhelpful emotion, for example an email or a comment from someone, then leave it for a while and go back to it when you feel calmer.
- **Talking to someone.** Your mentor will be helpful if they are around but you will find that other people are often willing to listen and may be able to offer helpful advice. Be mindful of other people's space though – it isn't recommended that you lunge at the first person you meet! Select carefully and ask if the other person has time for a quick chat. People are generally very understanding about the difficulties you will be facing – after all, they will have been through them themselves.

Emotional triggers

Figure 7.6 Mirror, mirror

We all have triggers for certain emotions which tend to provoke well-rehearsed responses. Some common triggers are:

- **Striving for perfection.** Getting frustrated if a lesson doesn't go well is normal but also remember that there is a lot to be learnt from your mistakes and a constant drive for perfection will simply make you feel inadequate. Think about it – *are you perfect?* I guess that 90 per cent of people will answer 'no' to that question (and the other 10 per cent may want to consider the traits of narcissism). *You are not perfect, we are not perfect, embrace the imperfection* and use it as an opportunity to continue to develop your practice.
- **Always trying harder.** If your students don't understand, you spend longer planning your lessons, if the 'stuff to do' list expands, you stay up later trying to get through it. This can become a vicious circle as it will simply make you more tired and in the long run less effective. *If what you are currently doing isn't working, don't do more of it – try something else.*
- **Staying strong.** The nature of working closely with other people means we feel we are letting others down if we don't do something. This can lead us to going to work when we are ill or not admitting it when we are struggling with something so that pressures begin to build up inside us. *Acknowledge your weaknesses and give yourself a break.*

Work-life balance

Figure 7.7 Work-life balance

Learning to become a teacher may be one of the most rewarding things you do. It is an emotional journey but also a very rewarding one. You will develop a lot of skills and learn new things, many of them about yourself. It is important that you make the most of the opportunity but it is also important to remember that this is not all there is. Other aspects of your life are what make you the person you are and in turn those interests and passions will make you a better teacher. Teaching can enhance your life and your life can enhance your teaching so it is very important that you make time for it. Some of the advice in this and other chapters will help you to organise your time more effectively and manage some of the emotions you will be experiencing. This should help to make the journey a more pleasant one but most of all it should allow you to make this a part, rather than the whole, of your life.

Things to think about

In this chapter we have explored the ways in which you can develop the skills of emotional resilience. Are there any situations you might find challenging? If so, which of the techniques covered in this chapter could you try? The only way to develop emotional resilience is through experience and practice so make a commitment to try something that will help you to develop positive thoughts and behaviours. We have included a goal-setting template at the end of the chapter so that you have somewhere to log some individual goals based on your reading of this and the previous six chapters.

In a nutshell

This resource can be photocopied and used as a revision tool or a prompt for discussion with your peers.

Self-efficacy

This describes a person's beliefs about their capability to exercise influence over their lives. The term was outlined by Bandura (1977) to explain the way our thoughts and feelings affect how we motivate ourselves to achieve outcomes. Bandura outlined the differences in the ways individuals might respond to events if they had a 'strong' or 'weak' sense of self-efficacy.

'Strong'	'Weak'
Problems seen as challenges Intrinsic interest in activities Sense of commitment to interests Recover quickly from setbacks Sustain efforts in the face of failure	Avoid challenging tasks Have lower aspirations Less commitment to goals See difficult tasks as beyond them Focus on personal failings and negative outcomes Less confidence in personal abilities

Source: Bandura (1977).

Putting it into practice

Whether you believe you can do a thing or not, you're right. This famous quote, accredited to Henry Ford, explains the concept of self-efficacy in a nutshell. Try the following to help develop your self-efficacy.

Take baby steps. If you see a task as overwhelming, break it down into small steps and enjoy the success of achieving each one.

Remember past success. If you think you can't do something . . . think about if there was a time when you could. Remember this success.

Visualise. Imagine yourself carrying out a particular task or behaviour successfully. See and feel what that is like – if you can visualise it, the chances are you can do it.

Recognise self-doubt. Notice self-doubt and accept it for what it is. This isn't a truth or a fact, it is simply a perception. If you can doubt yourself, you can also believe in yourself.

Get support. If you don't know where to start, talk to someone you trust. Ask what they would do then decide on your own approach.

Personal development goals

Use this space to set some initial goals for yourself. Don't be too ambitious – there will be plenty of time for that as your training progresses. Try to be specific, so think about what the goal will 'look like' when you have achieved it and how it will be measured.

Goals and Deadlines *(What do you want to achieve? By when?)*
Strategies *(How will you achieve these goals?)*
Success (How will you know you have achieved the goal(s)?)

Suggestions for further reading

Butler, G and Hope, T (2007) *Manage Your Mind: The Mental Fitness Guide,* 2nd edn. Oxford: Oxford University Press.

Goleman, G (1996) *Emotional Intelligence: Why It Can Matter More Than IQ*. London: Bloomsbury.

References

Bandura, A (1977) 'Self-efficacy: toward a unifying theory of behavioural change', *Psychological Review*, 84: 191–215.

Butler, G and Hope, T (2007) *Manage Your Mind: The Mental Fitness Guide,* 2nd edn. Oxford: Oxford University Press.

Ginott, H (1972) *Between Teacher and Child: A Book for Parents and Teachers*. New York: Macmillan.

Goleman, G (1996) *Emotional Intelligence: Why It Can Matter More Than IQ*. London: Bloomsbury.

Health and Safety Executive (2016) Available at: **https://hse.gov.uk** (accessed 23 April 2017).

Part 2

Your teaching practice

In this section you will be discovering the skills you need to make a success of your training. This will help you to plan your journey and use your time effectively.

The following chapters will explore:

- **ways in which you can work effectively with others;**
- **how to use feedback and self-reflection to enhance your development;**
- **strategies for overcoming barriers and developing your resilience.**

All of which will help you to make the most of the experience.

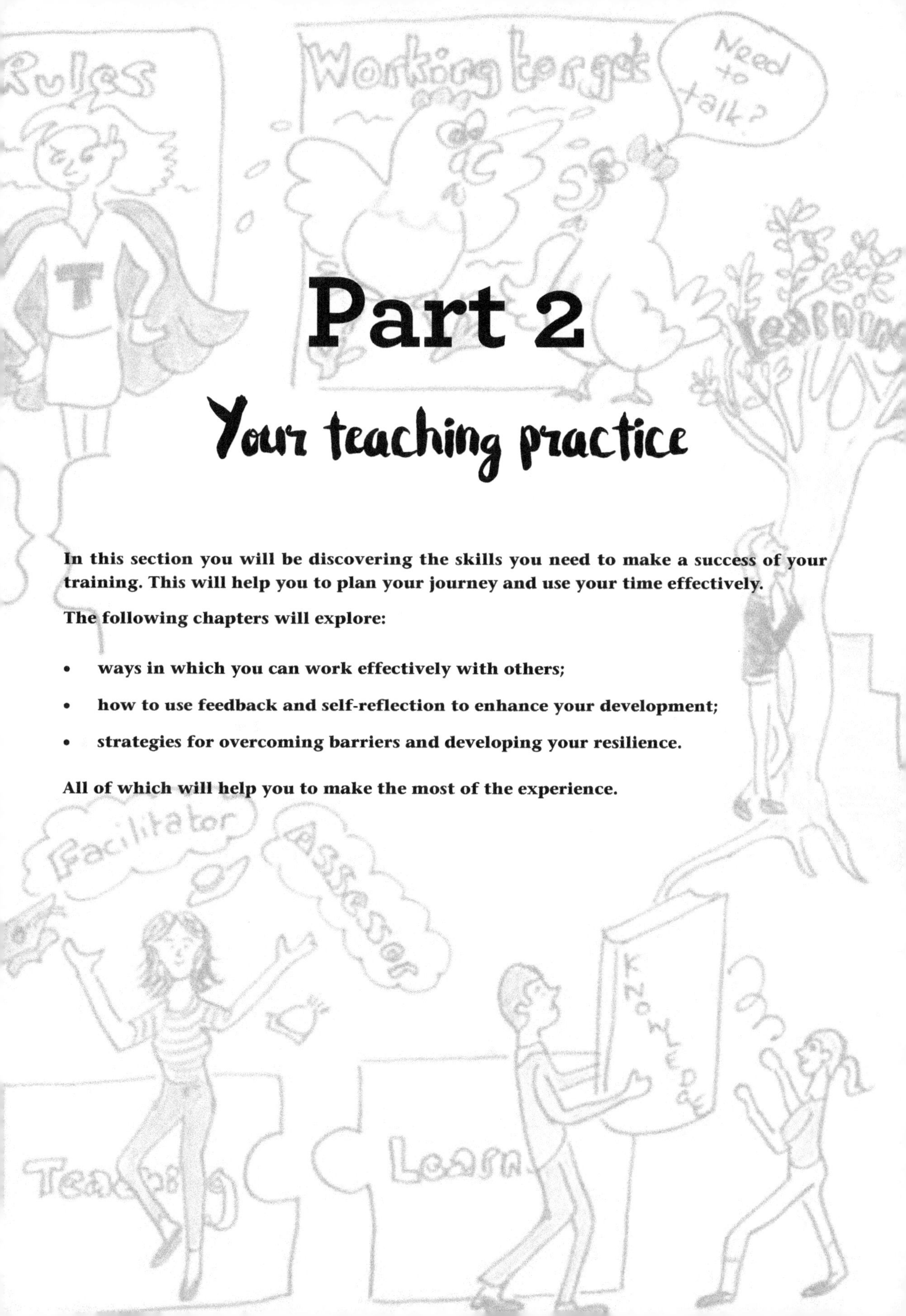

8

What do teachers DO?

In this chapter we will explore:

- **key aspects of the teacher's role;**
- **the differences between teaching and teacher competencies.**

Introduction

Figure 8.1 Hats

As you are beginning to discover in your training, teaching is a complex role making it difficult to describe in simple terms. You may be expected to wear several 'hats' in one day and be able to switch between these at a moment's notice. The scope of the teacher's role is too wide to explore everything in one chapter so we have focused on four key aspects of it: teaching, facilitating learning, assessing and using counselling skills. Perhaps the most fundamental aspect at this point in your career is the dual role you have undertaken as both teacher and student, and even when your training is complete we would argue that this will *and should* continue throughout your career as, ultimately, *The teacher is the one who gets the most out of the lessons, and the true teacher is the learner* (Elbert Hubbard, n.d.).

The role of the teacher

Figure 8.2 Knowledge

Traditionally the role of the teacher was seen as a supplier of information, the expert in a particular subject or topic. This presents an image of eager learners, seated in rows ready to soak up information, with the teacher at the front of the class passing on pearls of wisdom. This, of course, is far removed from the modern teacher's role which could more accurately be described as *teacher, facilitator, assessor, counsellor . . .* and much more. This multifaceted occupation calls for a more versatile approach, particularly when we consider that there are constraints and boundaries which must be accommodated. It is doubly difficult when this role is undertaken as a trainee on placement, when you are not necessarily aware of organisational limitations, or a trainee who is undertaking the dual roles of employed teacher and trainee teacher at the same time. The key to surviving this is being aware of potential difficulties, anticipating them and being prepared so that they are minimised. You can then focus on those things which will help you become the type of teacher you want to be.

Your role as a teacher

The role involves the planning of effective learning opportunities and includes thinking about the content of a particular lesson, how the lesson will be structured and how learning will be checked.

As outlined by Hattie (1999 and 2009), the factors which are deemed to have the greatest impact on learning include reinforcement, activity and corrective feedback, therefore a simple approach might be to ensure that each lesson includes these opportunities and base your planning on the premise that learning is an active process in which all parties participate. It is possible to structure your lessons on this basis using a standard lesson plan format and examples are likely to be offered by your tutors and mentors. This is useful as far as it goes but it is important to remember that all lessons will need to be adapted to meet the needs of the group and of the individuals within it, so sticking rigidly to a formula is unlikely to work. You must also take into account individual differences, group dynamics, the needs of the topic and so on.

There are regular changes in all aspects of education and to remain effective in your role you need to keep up to date with policy changes, educational research, and curriculum and assessment changes. It is also really important to keep pace with any changes in your specialist subject which could include new research or trends. Teachers who don't do this put themselves and their students at a disadvantage.

Activity

Make a list, or create a concept map, outlining all of the things you will need to keep up to date within your teaching role. For each of the items listed try to think of a strategy you can use to ensure you are as up-to-date as possible.

There are many ways to keep up to date and there is a vast array of information available to you – you just need to know where to find it. Some potential ideas are:

- Social media (such as Twitter) can provide daily updates and most organisations now have a Twitter account. If you are unsure of who to follow, have a chat to your tutors, mentors and peers for ideas. Many of them will use this as a medium for fast information. An important point to remember is that any social media will form part of your public profile. If you are going to use Twitter as a professional tool then you need to tweet a professional image.
- Journals and articles are really helpful in highlighting the latest research and this is essential in knowing what other people in your professional community are doing.
- Educational blogs are another helpful source of information and often include links to other useful sites.
- Conferences, seminars and webinars provide opportunities to learn about current research, ideas and changes. They are also a great way to network with others.
- Online communities can be helpful when you want to discuss your ideas or some new information so ask others if they can recommend any.

Using any of these ideas will help you to build a professional learning community which will be helpful to you throughout your career.

Your role as a facilitator

The role differs slightly from that of the teacher even though they are mutually dependent. The facilitation of learning is based on the premise that learning is an active rather than a passive process and is achieved by the organisation of a number of activities in which learners can participate during lessons. Within this it is important to be mindful of the need for students to reflect on what they have learnt and remember that a lesson crammed with interesting activities is engaging but may be confusing if no time is given to think about and connect different parts of the experience. Facilitating opportunities for experience, followed by reflection, will provide scope to make sense of new learning and consider how it might be transferred or adapted in different situations.

The following adaptation of Kolb's learning cycle provides an illustration of this process.

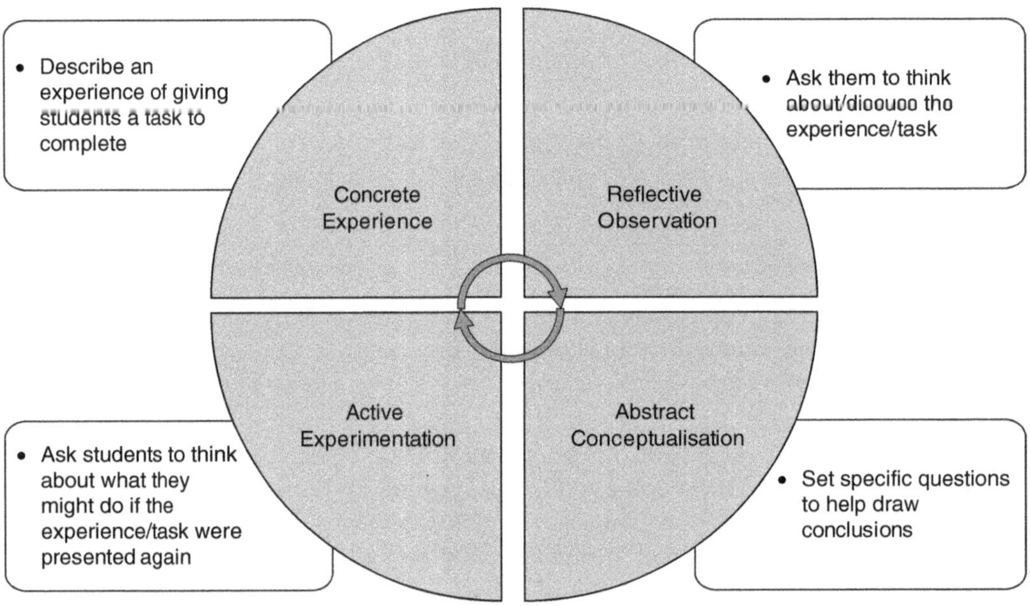

Figure 8.3 Kolb's learning cycle

The idea of teachers as facilitators is not a new one. It originated in the 1960s through the work of Carl Rogers and Josephine Klein and was based on the premise that learning was far more important than teaching, therefore the teacher's role was to create a positive environment in which learning could take place. Inevitably this also removes the emphasis from instruction and more didactic teaching methods such as presentations.

The learning cycle outlined in this chapter provides a structure from which to organise your lessons to enable you to facilitate learning. Although you could potentially start at any point, a logical beginning might be 'concrete experience' in which you would create an experience, for example a demonstration, experiment or a story – something which captures the essence of the lesson and creates 'food for thought'. If students are involved in an activity at this point, that will focus their attention. The next stage is to provide an opportunity for reflection – this could be achieved by using questions or generating a discussion. 'Abstract conceptualisation' is the point at which you are encouraging the students to make sense of the new information, so you might set specific questions which provide an opportunity to make links between this new information and things they might already know, for example: *What is similar and different about this? How does this compare to what we learnt about in the last lesson?* In a sense, this is about piecing together parts of the jigsaw. The active experimentation phase of the model is about transferring learning to new situations, so you could ask students to think about what they might have done differently or how the information could be used in a different context.

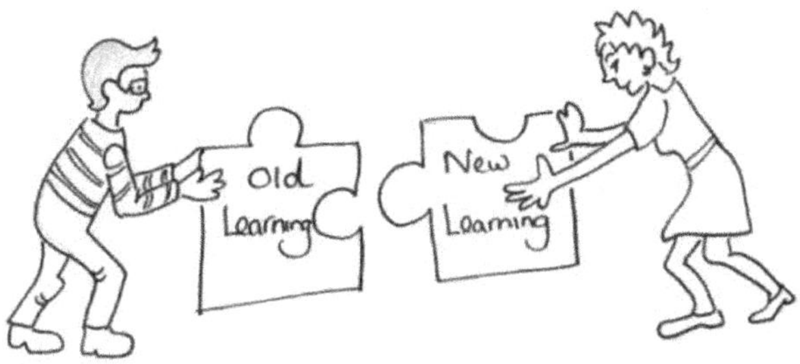

Figure 8.4 Constructing learning

There are myriad strategies you can use to facilitate learning which will help you to create a positive learning environment in which everyone is actively involved. Initially it may be difficult to relinquish some of the control you might be used to in a more traditional teaching context but this is something you will become accustomed to – it just takes practice. It is important that, whatever approach you take, you use a variety of teaching strategies and provide your learners with the opportunity not just to absorb information but to make sense of it. This will make the learning experience far more memorable and meaningful.

Your role as an assessor

The emphasis moves from creating learning opportunities to assessing what specific learning has taken place. Assessment is a key element of teaching; in fact, it could be argued that there is no teaching without assessment. We may teach something to the best of our ability, but if our students haven't learnt anything, then have we actually taught anything?

Figure 8.5 Blake cartoon strip

Source: Blake (1974).

Teaching and learning should be inseparable, therefore checking learning within each lesson is essential to good teaching practice. This doesn't mean that we have to implement formal tests or set essays every lesson – there is a variety of simple techniques you can use as learning checks, ranging from question and answer to quizzes, tests and short tasks. This is all part of formative assessment which we will cover in more detail in Chapter 15 but, put simply, this form of assessment is designed to promote students' learning and to provide teachers with information that allows them to alter their practice. It is the sort of assessment that is built into classroom practice and should form a significant part of everyday teaching as we need to ensure that not only are we teaching effectively but also effective learning is taking place.

Reflection

Think about the last class that you taught - what strategies did you use to check whether or not your learners had understood the content of the lesson? Do you consider these to be assessment methods?

It is likely that there are many things you do automatically and don't recognise the part they play in the assessment process. For example, how many times do you ask questions? Do you ever direct questions to particular learners? If so, why do you do that? Do you include games, quizzes and activities which go over the material you have covered? Do you give your students homework? Any one of these things is an assessment activity if it provides you with an opportunity to gain feedback on learning and the students an opportunity to get information on how they are doing.

Your role as a counsellor

One of the key considerations is to be aware of boundaries and remember that your role involves counselling skills but does not extend to counselling learners who may have more significant issues. Counselling skills are something you can and probably do use every day and centre around active listening. Active listening simply means that you are fully focused on what is being said rather than what you might contribute to the conversation. To develop your active listening skills, consider the following points.

- **Listen for main ideas** – the important points that the speaker wants to get across. Do one or two themes reoccur throughout? Are ideas or phrases repeated? Really listen for the themes – it is easy to make assumptions about what they are.
- **Let the speaker finish what they wanted to say before you speak** – this reassures the speaker that you are actually listening and, while it seems obvious enough, it is surprising how many people forget this simple point in their eagerness to add to the conversation.
- **Ask questions** – sometimes people are afraid of asking questions because they feel it gives the impression they haven't been listening. In fact, it is just the opposite. Questions show that you are

trying to understand what is being said, that you are clarifying meaning. They are a way of creating meaning for yourself, so, however silly the question seems, if it will help your understanding . . . ask.

- **Use paraphrasing** – you could summarise what you have heard in your own words and seek agreement or clarification. This shows the speaker that you have been listening and may help to put things into context, this is particularly true when the discussion centres around a problem or concern.
- **Be aware of your body language** – when listening actively, your physiology is very important – you listen with your whole body, not just your ears. It is essential to convey to the speaker that you are listening to them.

Figure 8.6 Paraphrasing

We will include more information on these skills in Chapter 16 as they are a significant part of any role which involves day-to-day interactions with others. Having an understanding of the ways in which you are able to offer support as well as the limitations of your role is essential to ensuring that your learners get the right professional guidance. It also ensures that you follow your own organisation's policy and adhere to the legislative processes which underpin this. Remember that boundaries are in place for good reason and should protect learners as well as teachers.

Activity

It is important to be aware of any policies relating to learner support and how you can signpost learners to these if required. Think about the potential issues learners might present you with, for example problems at school or outside school, difficulties in coping with work or getting on with others. List everything you can think of. Take this to the next meeting you have with your mentor and ask them where you can find the information about how and where to signpost learners should you need to.

Teaching roles do vary between organisations, particularly when it comes to specific tasks such as the completion of paperwork, so it is important to familiarise yourself with the scope and limitation of the role within your own context.

What should teachers do?

When you start your training it can be difficult to gain a clear perspective on the scope of the teacher's role. The multitude of books outlining what good teachers should do are of little help. As an example, the Wordle shown in Figure 8.7 was created by looking at a variety of how-to textbooks which outlined the teacher's role. Most of the words were premised with 'a teacher should . . .'.

Figure 8.7 Wordle

If we were to adopt the whole host of things outlined in the plethora of texts and guides, we would be in a constant spin just trying to keep up with it all. It is important to gain a sense of perspective early on.

The teaching role does include a number of responsibilities and knowing where to start can be overwhelming. The complexity of the role can be daunting but it is worth reminding yourself that it is manageable if your focus remains on the right things. What can be difficult sometimes is working out what the 'right things' are.

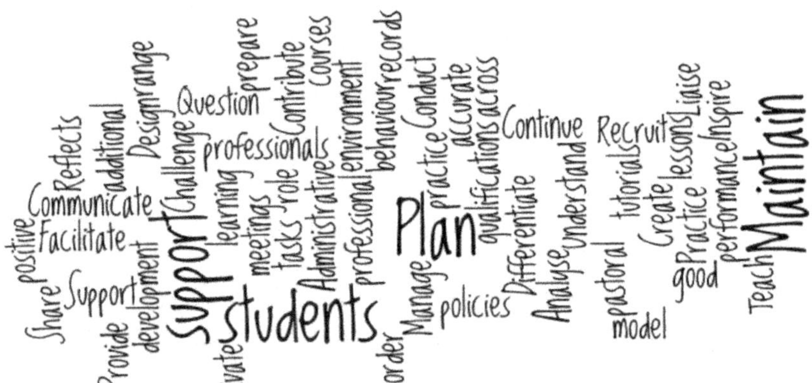

Teaching competences and teacher competences

When reviewing the overall requirements of the teaching role, the European Commission made a distinction between *teaching* competences and *teacher* competences (European Commission, 2013) defining the former as those things associated with the craft of teaching and the latter as those things which provide a more systemic view of teacher professionalism.

Based on this definition, teaching competences would include things like the following.

- planning lessons;
- presenting information;
- carrying out assessments;
- managing classroom behaviour;
- managing the overall lesson.

The development of teacher competences is not directly linked to classroom practice, although it will influence it. These competences are related to the profession overall and represent a dynamic combination of the range of skills involved in the process of becoming a teacher. Teacher competences would include things like the following.

- reflecting on teaching practice;
- testing out new ideas;
- collaborating with other professionals;
- developing your own professional identity.

Often the focus is firmly placed on the development of *teaching* competences rather than *teacher* competences and at a superficial level this does seem like a sensible approach. Developing classroom competence and confidence is essential if you are to feel comfortable in the role. However, to focus solely on this aspect of development would be short-sighted and will block your route to becoming an expert teacher. To fully understand the teacher's role, its scope and its potential impact, it is important to have an understanding of the bigger picture, to see the role from other perspectives and to reflect on it in an informed way. As suggested at the beginning of this chapter, teaching is not necessarily about knowing, it is more about being willing to learn, and the true teacher – the expert teacher – is always a learner.

Developing teacher competences requires a number of skills which have been summarised as follows.

- **Thinking** – which involves the critical examination of beliefs about teaching and professional practice as well as the ability to reflect on and adapt practice.
- **Knowing** – including subject knowledge and teaching skills. This includes learning about new technologies and creating an evidence base for practice by applying theory to methods.

- **Feeling** – relates to professional identity, attitudes, values and expectations. This includes self-efficacy as well as collaboration with others in order to achieve educational aims.
- **Acting** – which brings together many of these skills and involves integrating thoughts, knowledge and dispositions into practice.

Figure 8.8 Skills and competencies

Inevitably it takes time to develop the range of teaching and teacher competences outlined in this chapter but, with the right guidance and support, the process of becoming a teacher will prove to be a rewarding challenge.

Taking responsibility for the development of your knowledge and skills in relation to teaching is the first step to becoming a teacher. To make the most of your training, it is important to take charge and start thinking about the things you need to know or be able to do in order to be effective in the role. There is much more to learn but remember this is just the start of the journey. Taking each step in turn, mastering the skills and reflecting on your own learning is the key to your development.

Things to think about

Whether you are a trainee on placement, or a more experienced teacher in training, you will have gone into this with clear views on what the role entails. This may have been influenced by your own experiences of education or by your practical experience with students and other teachers. These things will have a significant impact on how you view the scope and potential of the role; it is equally important that previous ideas inform rather than limit your current understanding and that you question how your own perspective has developed. In doing so, you will have the opportunity to explore the full potential of the teacher's role and to generate new ideas about how to successfully adapt your understanding and practice in order to become an expert teacher. Have your ideas about the teacher's role changed after reading this chapter? Why is it important to recognise teacher competences as well as teaching competences?

Teaching competences and teacher competences

When reviewing the overall requirements of the teaching role, the European Commission made a distinction between *teaching* competences and *teacher* competences (European Commission, 2013) defining the former as those things associated with the craft of teaching and the latter as those things which provide a more systemic view of teacher professionalism.

Based on this definition, teaching competences would include things like the following.

- planning lessons;
- presenting information;
- carrying out assessments;
- managing classroom behaviour;
- managing the overall lesson.

The development of teacher competences is not directly linked to classroom practice, although it will influence it. These competences are related to the profession overall and represent a dynamic combination of the range of skills involved in the process of becoming a teacher. Teacher competences would include things like the following.

- reflecting on teaching practice;
- testing out new ideas;
- collaborating with other professionals;
- developing your own professional identity.

Often the focus is firmly placed on the development of *teaching* competences rather than *teacher* competences and at a superficial level this does seem like a sensible approach. Developing classroom competence and confidence is essential if you are to feel comfortable in the role. However, to focus solely on this aspect of development would be short-sighted and will block your route to becoming an expert teacher. To fully understand the teacher's role, its scope and its potential impact, it is important to have an understanding of the bigger picture, to see the role from other perspectives and to reflect on it in an informed way. As suggested at the beginning of this chapter, teaching is not necessarily about knowing, it is more about being willing to learn, and the true teacher – the expert teacher – is always a learner.

Developing teacher competences requires a number of skills which have been summarised as follows.

- **Thinking** – which involves the critical examination of beliefs about teaching and professional practice as well as the ability to reflect on and adapt practice.
- **Knowing** – including subject knowledge and teaching skills. This includes learning about new technologies and creating an evidence base for practice by applying theory to methods.

- **Feeling** – relates to professional identity, attitudes, values and expectations. This includes self-efficacy as well as collaboration with others in order to achieve educational aims.
- **Acting** – which brings together many of these skills and involves integrating thoughts, knowledge and dispositions into practice.

Figure 8.8 Skills and competencies

Inevitably it takes time to develop the range of teaching and teacher competences outlined in this chapter but, with the right guidance and support, the process of becoming a teacher will prove to be a rewarding challenge.

Taking responsibility for the development of your knowledge and skills in relation to teaching is the first step to becoming a teacher. To make the most of your training, it is important to take charge and start thinking about the things you need to know or be able to do in order to be effective in the role. There is much more to learn but remember this is just the start of the journey. Taking each step in turn, mastering the skills and reflecting on your own learning is the key to your development.

Things to think about

Whether you are a trainee on placement, or a more experienced teacher in training, you will have gone into this with clear views on what the role entails. This may have been influenced by your own experiences of education or by your practical experience with students and other teachers. These things will have a significant impact on how you view the scope and potential of the role; it is equally important that previous ideas inform rather than limit your current understanding and that you question how your own perspective has developed. In doing so, you will have the opportunity to explore the full potential of the teacher's role and to generate new ideas about how to successfully adapt your understanding and practice in order to become an expert teacher. Have your ideas about the teacher's role changed after reading this chapter? Why is it important to recognise teacher competences as well as teaching competences?

In a nutshell

This feature covers the essentials of Kolb's learning cycle and provides examples of how you can embed this into your practice. The resource can be photocopied and used as a revision tool or a prompt for discussion with your peers.

Kolb's Learning Cycle

This four-stage cycle is a key principle of experiential learning theory in which events provide a basis for reflection. Based on these individually experienced reflections, it is possible to 'conceptualise' or make sense of the learning, so that we might further adapt or experiment. The cycle is typically shown in four stages:

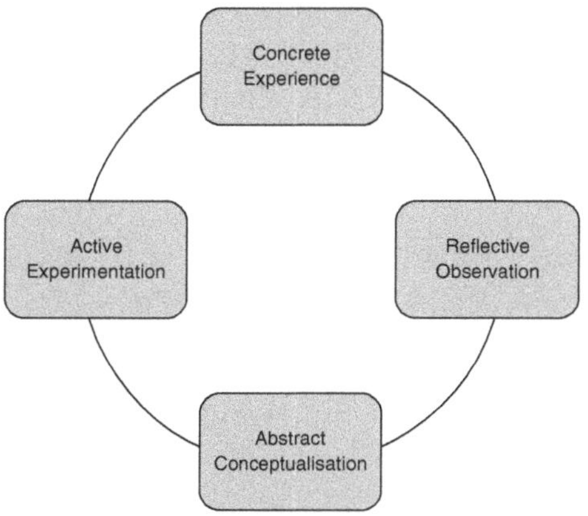

Source: Kolb (1984).

Putting it into practice

The model represents a cycle whereby learning goes through a number of stages; therefore, including all of these elements in your planning would ensure that learners have the opportunity to fully experience a new skill or concept. This adds depth to the learning event and provides 'food for thought' in terms of further development.

By including an experiential activity and a chance to reflect on this the lesson becomes much more valuable than simply learning a script. Different teaching and learning activities are appropriate for the various stages of the cycle – a few to think about are as follows:

Concrete:	Reflective:
Role play Simulation Games	Journals Discussion Metaphors
Abstract:	**Active:**
Lectures Journals Videos	Work experience Project Field work

Suggestions for further reading

European Commission (2013) *Supporting Teacher Competence Development for Better Learning Outcomes*. European Commission, July.

References

Blake, B (1974) 'I Taught Stripe to Whistle' [cartoon]. Available at: **http://alhsformativeassessment.blogspot.co.uk/2013/01/look-at-cartoon-linked-here-and-explain.html** (accessed 8 December 2017).

European Commission (2013) *Supporting Teacher Competence Development for Better Learning Outcomes*. European Commission, July.

Hattie, JA (1999) *Influences on Student Learning*. Inaugural professorial address, University of Auckland, New Zealand.

Hattie, J (2009) *Visible Learning: A Synthesis of Over 800 Meta-analyses Relating to Achievement*. London: Routledge.

Hubbard, E (n.d.). Available at *http://ecelebrityfacts.com/famous-elbert-hubbard-quotes-the-teacher-is-the-one* (accessed 23 May 2017).

Kolb, DA (1984) *Experiential Learning Experience as a Source of Learning and Development*. Englewood Cliffs, NJ: Prentice Hall.

9

Planning great lessons

In this chapter we will explore:

- **elements of great lessons;**
- **structuring lessons;**
- **strategies for encouraging critical thinking and curiosity.**

Introduction

He who fails to plan is planning to fail is a quotation which is frequently credited to Winston Churchill (during the Second World War) and is linked to many aspects of life. Planning great lessons is no exception. Detailed planning not only allows you to outline what you want to achieve in a given lesson but creates the opportunity to take a more flexible approach and work effectively with your students. This chapter considers the importance of planning lessons, dispels a few myths about what good lessons should contain and reviews a number of strategies in order to avoid the formulaic 'one size fits all' approach.

Myths about great lessons

It is not uncommon for teachers to adapt their teaching according to what is expected of them by others, including bodies such as Ofsted, or other teachers within their organisation. This is understandable given the prevalence of graded lesson observations as a form of quality assurance and performance management. However, it can also lead to the development of a rather formulaic approach to teaching in which certain things 'must' be done in order to evidence what is deemed by others to be 'good practice' (Thompson and Wolstencroft, 2014).

According to Harriet Harper (a former Ofsted inspector, 2013), there are a number of myths about what teachers 'must' do in lessons including the following.

Reading out learning outcomes at the start of every lesson

It is clearly a sensible approach to plan lessons according to learning objectives as this will ensure that your teaching has a genuine focus. We would also argue that this is information you should share with learners during the lesson but there appears to be no sound pedagogical reason why learning objectives must be stated at the beginning of every lesson, or indeed why they need to be revisited several times and 'ticked off' during a lesson. Remember that objectives are there as a guide for lesson content but they are set by the teacher. If your lessons are well structured and involve students, it is possible that you may even surpass your objectives as a result of the contributions of the group and, in this sense, sticking rigidly to them will constrain rather than enhance the learning taking place.

Producing perfect lesson plans

Lesson plans have a very specific purpose and are there to guide your teaching but too much emphasis on them will ensure that the focus is on teaching approaches rather than supporting learning. A lesson plan is a tool, it is not evidence of good teaching, therefore it should be treated as something which provides structure and support, not something which provides evidence of good teaching, and you should certainly deviate from it if required.

Insisting on group work

There is much research evidence to support the use of a collaborative approach to learning. However, actively involving students in lessons does not necessarily mean that you need to make everyone work in groups in every lesson. Group-based tasks are very helpful if they provide an opportunity for learners to engage effectively with the topic, but they are not valued by all learners and enforcing group work can be disruptive. It is also important to remember that group work needs to be carefully supervised to ensure that the activities do not generate misconceptions among students.

Frequently changing activities

The belief in changing activities frequently to sustain students' interest is something which has developed in line with a preference for active learning techniques. This is based on the premise that learners' interest will be maintained and that lessons will be considered 'fun'. This may be the case for some lessons and this approach may be appropriate for some topics, but it is not necessarily the case for everything and it is important that the methods used are aligned to the subject and the learning outcomes.

Always using technology

Technology can be used effectively to enhance lessons and is something which most learners will be familiar with. There are many resources to choose from and the use of mobile and tablet technologies in teaching is certainly a popular strategy. If this something that works well for your students and your subject then it is definitely something which will help you to develop innovative lessons, but, as with the use of group work, it is worth remembering that not all students respond well to this approach and that it can be overused in the same way as any other teaching strategy or resource.

Finally, we want to dispel one of the most damaging myths of all:

> *Others (including Ofsted inspectors) are better judges of your teaching than you are!*

One very important aspect of improving your teaching and increasing your students' learning is to develop an open and honest approach to evaluating your lessons. This will allow you to adapt strategies and continue to enhance your own teaching style. As far as how effective your teaching has been, you and your students are probably the most effective barometer, not someone who observes what you are doing for an hour (or less). So, before assuming that you have to address the 'good lesson tick-list' and organising your lessons according to what others think is good practice, take an honest look at your planning and teaching and ask your students to tell you their thoughts. This will provide you with genuine evidence of a lesson's effectiveness and will allow you to take control of your planning and your development. We have also outlined some strategies for effective reflective practice in Chapter 4.

Lesson structure – planning what and how to teach

There are many approaches and trends related to the planning of teaching and in recent years the addition of a number of 'added extras' to lessons has meant there is the potential to dilute the real content of the lesson. If teachers are too focused on embedding a range of additions to the lesson it can become confusing for students and can mean that teachers are spending too much time thinking about how to teach a plethora of additional skills. We have seen many long and detailed lesson plans which have a list of additional things to be included in this lesson, for example:

- Literacy
- Numeracy
- Team working
- Learning styles
- 'Every child matters'
- British values
- Health and safety
- Levels of learning
- Wellness
- Personalised learning
- ICT (and probably many more).

In most cases these are included in the form of a checklist so that you can outline what you will 'address' in the lesson. While we do acknowledge that many of these skills are important, we would argue that they should be embedded in the overall curriculum, rather than individual lesson plans. If you plan effectively you are in a position to exploit opportunities to explore some of the things listed above and should certainly be open to this but it is not recommended that you plan your lesson around them. As many organisations have a standard format for lesson plans you may well be expected to conform to the 'house style', in which case it is important that you ensure that your lessons have a very clear and distinct focus.

What should I include?

A common concern for new teachers is knowing what to teach and how to teach their subject. This is a very real concern but one which should be easy to address if you approach it in the right way. In most cases class teachers will be following a standard scheme of work for their subject. This is a longer-term planning document which outlines which lessons will be taught when and although formats may vary it may be as simple as the example in Table 9.1.

Table 9.1 An example from a scheme of work

Date/week	Learning outcomes	Activities and resources	Differentiation	Links to assessment
10 Nov (week 6)	Explore use of language to describe characteristics	Group work - 'a member of my family'	Alternative individual task	1.2, 1.3, 1.5

This provides an overview of the subject and should show how individual lessons build up to form the whole. The headings and layout may differ but usually a scheme of work will include:

- timings;
- learning outcomes;
- activities and resources;
- links to assessment.

The scheme of work has a focus on what you are going to teach and when you need to teach it. Although it does make some reference to activities and resources this is usually from an overall planning perspective; the specifics of how to teach are usually reserved for the lesson plan. That said, there is a growing trend in many contexts of combining these documents, particularly when they are used in electronic format. This means that the scheme of work will have much more detail than the example provided in Table 9.1 or will include hyperlinks to more specific information relating to a lesson. Whichever approach is taken, when you have this overview it is much easier to plan lessons at an individual level and begin to think about *how* you are going to teach them.

Activity

List all the things you need to know about planning for your teaching. For example, do you have to use a standard format for lesson plans? Is there a scheme of work you should be following? How do teachers link lessons to assessments? Create a concept map with your questions and your own ideas then arrange to see your mentor to go through this. This will provide an opportunity to get a head start on your planning.

How can I specify what students should learn?

It is possible that learning outcomes may well be outlined in your scheme of work but you should also be aware of how to write these for your own lessons. A very common approach to writing learning objectives is to state what learners should be able to do at the end of the lesson, and a useful tool for establishing levels is provided by Bloom's taxonomy (1956) (see Table 9.2). Put simply this outlines levels of learning alongside descriptors of activities which demonstrate this learning. In theory, the levels of learning increase in difficulty from knowledge to evaluation.

Table 9.2 A summary of Bloom's taxonomy

Level	Students will be able to:
Knowledge	Recall, list, describe, identify
Comprehension	Explain, interpret, discuss, summarise
Application	Use, apply, produce, show
Analysis	Review, analyse, deduce, differentiate
Synthesis	Compose, construct, create, design
Evaluation	Appraise, argue, assess, choose

Source: Bloom (1956).

Using this approach, if you were expecting your learners to outline the different parts of a formal letter you might use the following learning objective:

> *Students should be able to list the different parts of a formal letter* or . . . *state at least four parts of a formal letter . . .*

If your aim were to get your students to apply this learning you might use the following:

> *Students should be able to produce a formal letter . . .*

Or at a higher level:

Students should be able to review and analyse a range of formal letters and outline similarities and differences . . .

Figure 9.1 Bloom's Taxonomy

What order should things be in?

Structuring lessons appropriately is a key element of good planning. As with most things, a good lesson plan should have a clear beginning, middle and end, but while that is a suitable starting point, there are one or two other things to consider.

In Chapter 2 we explored the concepts of deep and surface learning in relation to your own learning journey. This should also be given consideration when planning your lessons. If you want your students to adopt 'deep' learning approaches then you need to build your lesson around opportunities which allow them to achieve this. As outlined in Chapter 2, deep learning is more likely to be achieved if students are able to link new learning to previous knowledge or experience and, in doing so, discover the key principles which can be transferred from one lesson to another.

One way of achieving this is through the use of an advance organiser, originally credited to Ausubel (1968) and based on the principle that orientation towards a new topic is much simpler if learners can see where it fits in with what they already know. An advance organiser is simply a way of achieving this and can take many forms, for example:

- a concept map which shows old and new knowledge;
- a story or metaphor;
- a gapped handout (revising old knowledge and introducing new concepts);
- a KWL chart (based on what did you **Know** about . . . what do you **Want** to know about . . . what did you **Learn** about . . .).

You can be creative about the strategies you adopt, just remember that this is not simply revision activity going over what students learnt in the previous lesson, it should act as a bridge between new learning and old.

Reflection

Helping students to make sense of and remember new information is a key part of your role. In what ways do you think using an advance organiser will help them to do this?

The content which forms the main part of the lesson should be clearly focused on the main learning aims, so this content allows you and your learners to demonstrate achievement of the lesson's objectives. The first consideration will be based around how you choose to get across the key points. This may be by teacher input (the length of which will depend on your students' maturity and attention spans) followed by opportunities for guided and independent practice. Although there is a range of 'formulae' around for structuring lessons, the most important consideration is that you select strategies which are appropriate for your subject and your students, not strategies which are linked to a 'one-size-fits-all' lesson approach.

Activity

The list in Table 9.3 (see page 100) represents ten of the most commonly used teaching strategies. Think about each one in relation to your subject and consider the advantages and disadvantages of the approach.

Being inclusive

In Chapter 11 we will explore the full extent of what it means to be an inclusive teacher; however, it is important to highlight inclusive practice in relation to lesson planning at this point. Inclusive teaching and learning can mean different things to different people but for the purposes of this chapter our definition relates to practice which does not exclude any learners within a group, as opposed to specific adaptations which may need to be in place for learners with specific needs.

Table 9.3 The ten most commonly used teaching strategies

Strategy	Description
Presentation	Providing information using a presentation tool such as PowerPoint or Prezi
Discussion	Putting students into small groups to discuss a given topic
Demonstration	Teacher demonstrates a skill or activity
Show and tell	This involves telling students what to do and showing them how to do it
Questioning	Teaching through asking rather than telling
Practical activities	Specific individual or group-based tasks
Peer teaching	Using students to teach each other
Telling stories	Using anecdotes or stories to illustrate key teaching points
Problem-solving	Using individual problem-solving tasks to generate discussion
Think/pair/share	Students outline individual thoughts on a question, discuss this with a partner, then with the wider group

In every lesson, it is important that we consider the various dimensions of diversity which may have an impact on how individuals will relate to the learning and to each other. These represent who we are, how we learn and how we might interact with others. Although there are many groupings to be found in relation to diversity, the following provides a simple outline of key factors:

- **Personality** – this relates to individual dispositions such as confidence, motivation, self-esteem, maturity, attitudes and behaviours.
- **Circumstances** – age, physical and mental ability, sexual orientation, gender.
- **Culture** – background, race, language, religion.
- **Education** – level/type of qualifications, skills, abilities, prior knowledge.

It is highly unlikely that your teaching will based on working with homogeneous groups of students, therefore an awareness of the ways in which you can create a respectful classroom environment which supports a diverse population of learners is key to successful planning.

Reflection

Think about the types of students you will be working with and the information you will need to allow you to plan inclusive lessons. Where can you find the information you need and how will you use this to ensure that your planning does not exclude any of your students?

Having high expectations

Being inclusive does not mean that you are 'going easy' on any individual learners. It simply means that you are removing anything which may disadvantage them. It would be very easy in your planning to 'play safe' and create lessons in which you know all students can easily achieve the specific learning objectives but it is very important that you also consider how you create a climate in which students want to achieve to the best of their ability – anything less is a missed opportunity.

The work of Rosenthal and Jacobson (1968) reinforced this point by carrying out experiments which highlighted how teacher expectations influenced student performance. Put simply, positive expectations influenced performance in a positive way, while negative expectations influenced performance negatively.

Figure 9.2 Pygmalion – 1

The phenomenon was originally described as the 'Pygmalion effect' based on George Bernard Shaw's play *Pygmalion* in which Professor Henry Higgins insists that he can take a cockney flower girl and, after training, pass her off as a duchess. This theory was based on the premise that:

> *When we expect certain behaviors of others, we are likely to act in ways that make the expected behavior more likely to occur.*
>
> (Rosenthal and Babad, 1985: 36)

Consciously or not we let people know what our expectations of them are. We exhibit thousands of cues – some as subtle as the tilting of the head or the raising of eyebrows but most are much more obvious – and people pick up on those cues. In a nutshell, this theory suggests:

- we form certain expectations of people or events;
- we communicate those expectations with various cues;
- people tend to respond to these cues by adjusting their behaviour to match them;
- the result is that the original expectation becomes true.

Figure 9.3 Pygmalion – 2

Critical thinking

One way of promoting high expectations in the classroom is to encourage students to think critically about what they are learning. This can be a difficult skill to develop as it often involves the teacher relinquishing a bit of control over the management of the lesson – logically, if you are going to encourage your learners to think critically, they will apply this skill to all information that is presented to them. According to Brookfield:

> *When people think critically they try to identify the assumptions that frame their thinking and actions, and they try to check out the degree to which these assumptions are accurate and valid. The chief way they do this is by looking at their ideas and decisions from several different perspectives.*
>
> (Brookfield, 2013: 21)

Developing critical thinking skills allows students to systematically process information and generally aids understanding. This means that skills such as conceptualising, analysing and synthesising are enhanced as students strive to make sense of rather than simply regurgitate information.

Figure 9.4 Critical thinking

Some popular strategies for developing critical thinking are compare and contrast activities, brainstorming and probing assumptions. Another strategy might be to ask students to put together an 'assumptions inventory' (Brookfield, 2013) based on information you are presenting to them. This would involve you presenting an idea or a concept then asking the students to explore the assumptions behind your presentation by considering what assumptions had guided the choice of information to present and what other perspectives could have been included.

Encouraging curiosity

An environment which promotes critical thinking should also be one which encourages curiosity and a love of learning. While we would argue that it is difficult to plan for this, detailed planning will allow you the freedom to explore your students' curiosity and generate a classroom culture in which questions are asked, discussed and explored in depth.

Curiosity could be described as the pursuit of new knowledge – if we are curious we are generally not satisfied with what we already know or have been told. It is that willingness to explore that defines the curious student, this makes curiosity closely connected to learning as it is a source of motivation.

It is also something which takes practice, alongside a willingness to be open to new ideas, as articulated by the White Queen from *Alice's Adventures in Wonderland*:

> *'There's no use trying,' she said. 'One can't believe impossible things.'*
>
> *'I dare say you haven't had much practice,' said the Queen. 'When I was your age I always did it for half an hour a day. Why, sometimes I believed as many as six impossible things before breakfast.'*
>
> (Carroll, 1865)

Figure 9.5 Curiosity

Like Alice, many students may be reluctant to explore new learning, so how do we generate a sense of curiosity? Largely this is down to the learning climate you create through your approach to teaching. By being openly curious yourself you are modelling the behaviours of curiosity; by asking and encouraging questions you are creating an open environment in which discussion and exploration can take place. It is also important to ensure that learners feel 'safe' within the classroom, particularly in the sense of emotional safety which can be encouraged by having classroom rules which enhance the importance of demonstrating mutual respect. Some initial strategies you could try are:

- revisiting old questions from a different perspective;
- encouraging play through different approaches and a sense of fun;
- creating a climate in which collaboration is the norm;
- avoiding following formulae . . . introducing unpredictable content and different teaching methods.

Create a learning environment which is multi-sensory, so that students can learn through a variety of senses, for example through sound, sight and touch.

Checking learning

It is important that you also plan opportunities to ensure that learning is taking place during your lessons and we would stress that your planning should take account of this. It is important to check learners' progress regularly to assess whether or not anyone is having difficulty with the lesson content and to ensure that you find ways of overcoming any obstacles to learning. There is a range of simple strategies you can use including tests, activities and questioning – the key message is to ensure that you check learning at several points within a lesson, not just at the end. We will cover this in more detail in Chapter 15.

Lesson planning structures and paperwork

A lesson plan can be seen as a sequential guide to what the teacher wants to achieve within a given lesson and something which will help keep the lesson on track. However, a good lesson plan is never too rigid or so detailed that it is difficult to follow when you are in the classroom. Every teacher should go into a lesson with a plan of what they want to achieve – in effect this represents your lesson objectives and it is important that careful thought is given to the content and structure of the lesson. However, it is also important that you have the confidence to move away from your lesson plan should the need arise.

There are a number of templates you can use to create a lesson plan and it is possible that you will be asked to work with a specific type. This should not be restrictive – you simply need to make it work for you.

The key aspects of any lesson are:

- clear learning aims;
- opportunities to revisit previous learning;
- a range of teaching strategies and resources;
- effective learning checks;
- opportunities for learners to be challenged;
- activities which create an inclusive learning environment in which every learner can achieve.

How you go about documenting this is up to you (although it may be worth checking if there is 'official paperwork' you need to use). Your plan should be simple and effective and the effort you expend on this should be on planning that is, thinking about how to structure the lesson so that it is the most effective learning opportunity rather than creating a beautiful lesson plan.

Things to think about

In what ways can lesson planning impact on learning? Now that you have an insight into key aspects of planning, are there any strategies you could employ to ensure that your planning is detailed and focused on learning? In what ways do you think you could improve your approach to planning?

In a nutshell

This feature covers the essentials of Bloom's taxonomy for the cognitive domain and provides examples of how you can embed this into your practice. The resource can be photocopied and used as a revision tool or a prompt for discussion with your peers.

Bloom's taxonomy cognitive domain

Blooms' taxonomy was originally created to promote higher forms of thinking in education (such as analysing and creating), rather than remembering facts (rote learning). It is now widely used in the creation of educational objectives and in the design of learning tasks. The diagram below shows the different levels of the taxonomy, showing those with increasing difficulty at the apex of the pyramid.

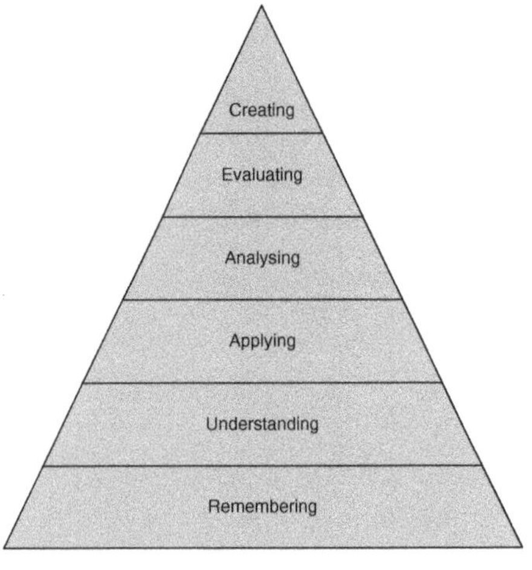

Source: Bloom (1956).

Putting it into practice

Teachers can use this in a variety of ways in order to create different levels of challenge for students. Three important ways in which you could use this are in the design of learning programmes, in-class activities and assessments.

Designing learning programmes Create a structure which increases in level of difficulty and ensures that students master the key facts before moving on to the next level. This also ensures that the higher levels are not neglected and that students don't get stuck in simply remembering things so that they can be applied.
Designing in-class activities Have a range of mastery tasks (those relating to remembering) that all students can achieve to build confidence. Introduce developmental tasks (such as analysing, transferring learning from one situation to another, creating new ideas). You can also differentiate for students at different levels in the same class.
Designing learning checks These could be questions at different levels, 'tell me the names of . . .?' or 'how might this be applied to . . .?' Learning checks can also take the form of games, quizzes and activities, all of which can include checks on different levels of learning.

Suggestions for further reading

Harper, H (2013) *Outstanding Teaching in Lifelong Learning*. Maidenhead: Open University Press

References

Ausubel, DP (1968) *Educational Psychology: A Cognitive View*. New York: Holt, Rinehart & Winston.

Bloom, BS (1956) *A Taxonomy of Educational Objectives: The Classification of Educational Goals, Handbook 1: Cognitive Domain*. Ann Arbor, MI: Longman Green.

Brookfield, S (2013) *Powerful Techniques for Teaching Adults*. San Francisco: Jossey-Bass.

Carroll, L. (1865) https://www.goodreads.com/work/quotes/17240250-through-the-looking-glass-and-what-alice-found-there

Harper, H (2013) *Outstanding Teaching in Lifelong Learning*. Maidenhead: Open University Press.

Rosenthal, R and Babad, EY (1985) 'Pygmalion in the gymnasium', *Educational Leadership*, 43 (1): 36–9.

Rosenthal, R and Jacobson, L (1968) *Pygmalion in the Classroom*. New York: Holt, Rinehart & Winston.

Thompson, C and Wolstencroft, P (2014) 'Give 'em the old Razzle Dazzle – surviving the lesson observation process in further education', *Research in Post-Compulsory Education*, 19 (3): 261–75.

10

Creating teaching resources

In this chapter, we will explore:

- **types of teaching resources;**
- **how to use resources effectively.**

Introduction

Creating teaching materials is one of the most time-consuming yet ultimately satisfying activities a teacher can undertake. If you want to create a positive and active learning environment then it is essential that you guide your students by providing high-quality teaching resources. In the staffroom and in your training, you will often hear phrases such as 'discovery learning', 'facilitation' and 'experiential learning'. They are all related to making sure that students find out the answers themselves. In effect, your role is as a support to this learning and this is where your resources can help.

Figure 10.1 Scaffold

Lev Vygotsky talked about the need to traverse the Zone of Proximal Development (ZPD) when learning. This refers to *the distance between the actual developmental level as determined by independent problem solving and the level of potential development as determined through problem solving under adult guidance, or in collaboration with more capable peers* (Vygotsky, 1978: 86). This is similar to the old adage: *Give a man a fish and you feed him for a day. Teach a man to fish and you feed him for a lifetime.* This also holds true in teaching. Telling students the answers means that they get the question right, helping them get to the answer might mean that they gain the skills needed to work out a range of answers themselves without resorting to needing your help. In this chapter, we will outline how high-quality teaching materials can facilitate this process and how it is important not to become reliant on just one group of resources.

Before deciding on the materials that we are going to use in our lessons there are a few questions that we need to ask ourselves. The answers to these questions will help you decide what materials are best suited for you.

- **Original or pre-prepared?** (Also known as the dangers of the internet bearing gifts.) There are a LOT of pre-prepared materials available. Some are carefully crafted and have a price tag to match, others are given away free via numerous sources on the internet. As with everything available online, the quality is variable. There are many gems available that can be used with little modification in your own teaching; however, it always pays to be wary of any resources that you did not make yourself. Ask yourself whether it meets your needs and check the accuracy of the material rather than trusting the answers. A good way of getting pre-prepared material is to join subject-specific groups on the internet. The *Times Educational Supplement* (**tes.com**) is a rich source of material while helpful and supportive groups, such as #teamenglish on Twitter, have sprung up on social media. Just remember, getting pre-prepared materials can help your workload enormously if you get it right, but if you use the wrong materials, there can be long-term implications.
- **ICT or not?** (And the importance of Plan B.) There is one irrefutable law in teaching and that is if something can go wrong with technology, it will – and normally at the worst possible moment. While this is often rather annoying, it need not be disastrous if you plan in advance. A good idea is to make sure that you include a Plan B on your lesson plan wherever you have indicated that you are going to use new technology. Having spare handouts, flipchart paper or ensuring that the lesson is flexible enough to move the non-ICT part of the session to the start, giving you time to solve the problem while students are working are all good ways of dealing with the panic caused by the failure of technology.

Activity

Imagine that you are teaching a group of Year 10 students. The topic is revision and you have prepared a detailed Microsoft PowerPoint presentation outlining the key points of the subject. Unfortunately, two minutes before the start of the lesson, you realise that the projector is broken and cannot be fixed in time for the session.

Think about what you would do in this situation.

- **When should materials be distributed?** There is no straightforward answer to this question as it depends on a range of different factors. The topic is one of those factors (so if you are teaching maths you might withhold the answers until students have tried the questions) but the most important factor remains the group that you are teaching. With some groups, handing out the materials at the end of the session encourages them to focus on what you are saying rather than assuming that all the answers are in the handout that you have provided for them, but other groups favour a different approach. Giving material out, either at the start of the class or before the lesson begins, can encourage students to learn about the topic before you start to teach which means that they can engage in discussion from the start of the session. One example of this is setting up a 'flipped classroom'. This is where you give students the information prior to the class and then encourage students to use this information in the classroom to understand the topic. This means that the lesson becomes more learner centred, or to utilise the phrase Alison King, often viewed as the architect of the idea, used, the students are able to construct meaning from the information rather than just being passive receivers of information (King, 1993).

Types of teaching resources

There is a much-quoted maxim in the literature that there are seven basic plots and all stories fall into one of these categories. Booker (2004) classified this theory by suggesting seven titles that could be used for these plots. These are:

Figure 10.2 Overcoming the monster

- overcoming the monster (for example, *Jaws* is about defeating a killer shark);
- rags to riches (an example might be *Cinderella* or *My Fair Lady*);
- the quest (in the *Lord of the Rings* there is a very clear end goal);

- voyage and return (*The Wizard of Oz* involves a journey to a magical world and the return);
- comedy (there are numerous examples but *A Midsummer Night's Dream* would fall into this category);
- tragedy (such as *Macbeth* or *Romeo and Juliet*);
- rebirth (again, a historical example might be *A Christmas Carol*).

Figure 10.3 Journey and return

Authors and directors tended to have a favourite category and, although they might sometimes deviate from this, they tend to return to it as it is seen to provide a safety net for them.

This approach can also be applied to the production of teaching materials where there are seven broad categories of resources:

- artefacts
- games
- manipulable kinaesthetics
- practical experiments
- problem-solving tasks
- peers (group tasks and challenges)
- adaptable ICT tools.

There is a tendency in teaching to use the same types of resources for each lesson with some teachers producing lesson plans that have a focus on handouts, others using presentation software to the exclusion of all other forms of communication, while others might rely on kinaesthetic resources. As with plots, it is possible to categorise all materials into seven basic categories, each of which has its own advantages and disadvantages. This does not mean that every material in each category is the same; it refers more to the fact that the basic ingredients are the same.

Reflection

Write down all the materials you have used so far in your teaching career. Do you seem to have a preference for certain types of resources and are there any obvious gaps in your resources (so, for example, do you never use ICT resources or alternatively have you underused the standard textbook)?

We will now look at each of the seven categories in turn. At the end of each section there will be a chance for you to reflect on the materials discussed and how you can adapt them to ensure that they 'stay fresh'.

Artefacts

The dictionary definition of an artefact refers to something made or given shape by 'man'. In a teaching context, it is simply an alternative resource for getting across information. The artefact is not simply a teaching resource, it is a representation of a topic, so if someone looked at the artefact they should have some idea about what you are trying to 'say' with it. So, for example, an object recreating hieroglyphics can be used in a lesson to help students learn about language but also life in ancient Egypt, as it would depict various objects common in the culture without you having to 'spell it out'.

Artefacts can be used in two ways. You can give students an artefact and ask them to use it to create something from it, or discuss how it might be used. These approaches encourage a cognitive or a social learning approach whereby students are thinking for themselves (the cognitive part) and working with others to decipher the learning (social learning). We will look at these theories in more detail in Chapter 12. This works well as students are encouraged to think for themselves and also to realise that there are often multiple interpretations of meaning rather than a narrow understanding which sometimes occurs when more teacher-centred materials are used.

Asking students to create an artefact works well with some groups. It can be a challenging activity but for more able (and creative) students it means that you can get them to think about a topic in far more depth than you normally would. Asking students to present their results can also be a good addition to the class as it will encourage them to use communication skills as well as the cognitive skills the artefact will give them.

Reflection

Think about the role that you have taken as a teacher in your last few lessons. Have you been the 'sage on the stage or the guide on the side' (King, 1993)? If the former, consider how you might change that role and give students the freedom to discover things for themselves.

Consider how the use of an artefact might facilitate this process.

Games

Using games as a part of your teaching materials can have the great advantage of engaging the competitive instinct of students. This can encourage a sense of fun in the class which, when channelled in the right direction, can mean that students enjoy the learning.

You can use any game as the basis of an idea – indeed the only limit is your imagination. Some popular examples are based on Bingo and Snakes and Ladders while others are ICT-based and use well-known television programmes like *Who Wants to Be a Millionaire?* or *Eggheads* as templates. Games are particularly good at encouraging a behaviourist approach (this refers to the reinforcement of concepts or ideas and is discussed in more detail in Chapter 12) as well as a social learning approach (providing opportunities for students to learn from each other).

As with all materials, there are problems with using this approach. Finding games that engage the complete class can be challenging and as many games are team-based some students are able to 'hide' during periods when games are being used. These activities also need to be kept under control as it is very easy for students to become overly stimulated leading to noise and disruption.

As with many teaching materials, the initial time spent making the resources can be extensive but, when they work well, games can be a powerful tool.

Reflection

As mentioned, the time taken to produce games can be offputting to teachers. One way of avoiding this is to produce a game that is transferrable to many different classes. So, the basics stay the same (for example the board used, the ICT framework put in place) but the specifics, perhaps the questions or the diagrams, change according to the group. Think about games that you could use in your teaching that are transferrable across classes.

Manipulable kinaesthetics

This is a simple example of a kinaesthetic activity which involves giving students something they can manually manipulate, for example a set of cards to sort into a specific order. This could be based on a logical order to provide structure or ranking activities which might generate discussion. As with the artefact this has the advantage of giving students control of the class, allowing them to discover things for themselves rather than you taking the lead role all the time.

Manipulable kinaesthetics work best when used to reinforce an activity or when introducing a new concept. Using these materials as reinforcement means that you can see if students understand a topic and something as simple as a card-sorting exercise means that you can run a plenary session without always having to use the standard question and answer technique.

Using manipulable kinaestethics can be a good way of engaging learners with a new topic and also to assess their previous knowledge. This ensures that a cognitivist approach can be used with students thinking through the topic rather than just learning the answers by rote.

Activity

Manipulable kinaesthetics can be a valuable form of materials but it is easy to fall into a pattern of using the same resources again and again. Think about examples of the type of materials you have used before and then think about new variations which would help your teaching.

Practical experiments

When we think about practical experiments, it is tempting just to think about science experiments but the reality is that they can be used in a variety of ways and provide opportunities for learners to construct and test out hypotheses in a controlled environment. As with the artefacts, this engages both cognitive and social learning theory to encourage students to take control of their learning.

An example of a practical experiment would be asking students 'can you form . . .?', and then giving them the name of a shape and some modelling clay. Hence students are encouraged to create (say) a square or circle. The advantage of this sort of resource is it is relatively easy to differentiate by ability. Stronger students can be given more challenging hypotheses (so they will need to create a pyramid or a sphere) while weaker students would be given more basic tasks such as creating a square.

Practical experiments often work well in bonding groups together and so might be used at the start of the course. Getting students to work as a team means that they can get to know each other and can be a useful way of breaking down barriers that exist between cliques in classes.

Reflection

Ensuring differentiation is a good way of making sure that you keep all students engaged in the learning but it does have some drawbacks. When done in an obvious manner it can create divisions and resentment in the classroom. Weaker students perceive themselves as inferior while stronger students might wonder why they are doing more difficult tasks. Think of ways in which you can differentiate your teaching materials without making it obvious to students what you are doing.

Problem-solving tasks

Problem-solving tasks are linked to practical experimentation but cover a much wider range of materials. The idea behind using this category is to get students to think creatively and apply this in a practical sense. A typical example of a problem-solving task would be a case study or scenario that generates discussion and alternative viewpoints.

The difference between this category and the practical experimentation category is that there is no hypothesis present with problem-solving tasks; this encourages greater creativity and also encourages students to apply theory learnt in lessons to practical examples. This transfer of learning might happen in a social learning environment which has the added benefit of encouraging a group approach.

Figure 10.4 Problem-solving

When using problem-solving activities it is important to ensure that students have some guidelines to follow (or support when completing the tasks) but when handled skilfully a teacher can use this approach to ensure students are able to explore concepts for themselves without being told the answer.

Reflection

When using problem-solving materials a key point is that the teacher should not tell the students the answer unless all else has failed. This can be a challenge when you see students heading in the wrong direction when trying to solve a problem.

Think of ways in which you would guide students towards the answer. Consider the wording of feedback and also the way in which you balance encouragement with ensuring that they successfully find a resolution.

Peers (group challenges)

This may be an opportunity to make use of peer teaching, discussion and debate. You can base this on thought-provoking activities or information that needs to be analysed and broken down. It may be an opportunity for students to evaluate something and take into account different perspectives.

One classic example of this is a balloon debate. This involves a group looking at a particular problem and bringing their own views and approaches to the task. This helps students realise that there are different perspectives (or frames of references, to link back to Chapter 5) when looking at tasks, a key skill to learn when fully evaluating a problem.

Figure 10.5 Balloon

Alternative peer group challenges focus on practical tasks. Examples of these are the egg drop experiment, where you provide an egg and various materials and encourage students to find creative ways of dropping an egg without breaking it, and the newspaper tower, whereby groups are given plentiful supplies of newspaper and have to build as tall a tower as possible. Again, the focus here is on social learning with students coming together to learn from each other and see things from alternative points of view.

Reflection

Practical experiments can bond groups together. Think of ways in which you can encourage students to work together rather than as individuals. This can create a group ethos and help prevent cliques. Reflect on ways in which you can do this within your groups.

Adaptable ICT tools

The use of ICT materials is such an everyday occurrence for most teachers that it seems strange to include it as part of the list of materials but the reality is that we tend to take ICT for granted and there is an inclination to do the same thing each lesson. Microsoft PowerPoint is a valuable tool but there are other useful tools such as Prezi or Spark. Using alternatives can give a fresh look to your teaching as well as encouraging you to try something new.

With the constant evolution of new technology, trying something new on a regular basis is key. One area that adaptable ICT tools can be very beneficial in is in the assessment of learning. Kahoot, Top Hat and other software are excellent ways of checking on knowledge in an interactive manner.

Activity

To avoid reusing the same ICT tools, a good activity to try is to select an area that you are teaching for a half term (so approximately six weeks) and then use a different ICT tool each week. It doesn't always have to be to do with presenting material. It might be connected to the assessment or a research tool, but it does mean that you learn a different ICT application each week.

Try it and see if it works for you.

Things to think about

This chapter is intended to help you to think about the teaching materials that you use and to stop you falling into the trap of using the same type of materials again and again. So, think about the following. Do you tend to use the same category of materials for each of your lessons? If yes, why is this? Is it possible for you to try different materials rather than relying on the same categories? Are there any new skills you need to develop before using any of the materials?

In a nutshell

This resource can be photocopied and used as a revision tool or a prompt for discussion with your peers. It is designed to help you think about one particular theory associated with the design and use of resources.

Using resources to flip the classroom

The idea of a flipped classroom (King, 1993) can be a daunting one for new teachers but the benefits can be significant when it runs smoothly.

The main idea is that students work on the basics of the topic before they attend the class and this means that they can focus on mastery of the concepts during the lesson.

Examples of this might be giving students reading or exercises to complete before the start of the lesson and then testing students when they come to the lesson to see what areas they are struggling with.

There are variations to this approach with groupwork suggested by some writers as a way of helping students learn in a social learning scenario prior to the teacher's input. Alternatively, online courses have been used by some tutors to engage with learners prior to the start of the session.

Source: King (1993).

Putting it into practice

Think of a topic that you will be teaching in the next few weeks.

⇩

Identify one part of the topic that you could teach by 'flipping' the learning and give students a task to encourage them to learn about it.

⇩

Using any ICT application set up a blog where students can contribute their thoughts about the topic.

⇩

Use the issues raised on the blog to inform your lesson and see if students are more engaged and performing better.

Suggestions for further reading

Ralston Ogles, M and Bogan, B (2014) *Flipping the Classroom – Unconventional Guide to Constructing the Classroom of the Future*. Murfreesboro, TN: UCM.

References

Booker, S (2004) *The Seven Basic Plots*. London: Bloomsbury.

King, A (1993) 'From sage on the stage to guide on the side', *College Teaching*, 41 (1): 30–5.

Vygotsky, LS (1978) *Mind in Society: The Development of Higher Psychological Processes*. Cambridge, MA: Harvard University Press.

11

The inclusive teacher

In this chapter, we will explore:

- **what is meant by inclusivity;**
- **how to take into account the needs of individual students;**
- **the importance of knowing your students.**

Introduction

When we start teaching there is a tendency to view groups as homogeneous entities that can be described using broad brush strokes. In the staffroom, it is not uncommon to hear teachers talking about a 'very good Year 9 group' or a 'Year 11 that needs to work harder'. The truth, of course, is rather more nuanced than that. A group is made up of a collection of individuals, all of whom are different and all of whom need to be taken into account when teaching.

That is not to say that the collective isn't important. As individuals interact with each other, certain norms start to appear within a group and that can give rise to the belief that a group has its own identity. Whyte (1952) suggested that groups can start behaving in similar ways, a process he called groupthink, but the reality is that within any class you will have a range of different individuals, all of whom will have different needs and motivators.

This chapter is about the process of ensuring that all students are included in the learning process.

What is inclusivity?

The National College for Teaching and Leadership defines inclusivity as an approach that stresses equity and inclusion of everyone in the classroom, irrespective of any special educational needs. The easiest way of demonstrating what is meant by inclusion is to think about your best friend and then try to define them in three words. This is a tricky task and one that can be immensely frustrating as you find yourself compromising over certain characteristics and simplifying their attributes in order to fit in with the task. It is the same with inclusivity: often we talk about the need to be inclusive but then define learners with reference to a very narrow range of features. We are all multifaceted and so to try to integrate everyone into the class is doomed to failure as it is not possible to address all the needs within the class.

Figure 11.1 Inclusivity

Nevertheless, addressing some of the most common inclusivity needs remains a key challenge for any teacher. While some specific needs may be highlighted formally, there are others which are more 'hidden' providing further challenges for planning lessons. This is where knowing your students becomes vital. The first term of any academic year is a time when this can be done. Make sure that you learn, not only the names of students but also their own individual needs so that these can be considered when you are planning lessons.

Reflection

This example considers a teacher who fails to differentiate between learners. Read through the case study and reflect on the problems at the end.

As Tom takes one final look at his lesson plan he is pleased with what he sees: the subject, Art GCSE, is his favourite and he has selected a famous painting from Van Gogh for the students to analyse. He checks that it has been copied correctly on to his presentation slides, checks that he has enough paper for the class to write their thoughts on and checks that the resources for the group plenary, which encourages students to work together to solve five questions about the life of the famous painter, are in place. Pleased that everything is prepared and ready, he opens the staffroom door and strides purposefully towards the classroom.

Two hours later Tom is slumped at the front of the room. As the bell goes, he looks at each of the students as they leave the room and reflects on the lesson. Ravi leads the way. Bright, interested and on course for a top grade, he became more and more disengaged as the class went on until, ten minutes from the end, frustration got the better of him and he shouted at his group-work partner, Emily, until she started crying. He knows she struggles with the class but she does try and she didn't deserve the abuse that she received.

Victor mutters the word 'discrimination' as he leaves the room. Tom shudders. How could he have known about his belief structure and how that would impact on the lesson? As he strains to hear what Victor is saying, Tom hears another voice; it is Marco saying that he will send a link that will help him understand his dyslexia. Nodding without thinking, Tom's eyes dart between Mariam, the class clown who has made his life hell for the last two hours, and Kasia whose limited grasp of English meant that she just kept repeating the words that Mariam told her to say, much to the amusement of the whole class.

Where did it all go wrong? Think about all the various needs that have been identified in the case study above and reflect on what you would have done differently.

The case study demonstrates how easy it is to misjudge planning when you don't know your students very well. We will now consider the story from the perspective of the members of the class.

Ravi's story – stretching the most able

Ravi stomped out of the class feeling as though the whole lesson had been a waste of his time. He was determined to get an A* in each of his GCSE exams and he could not see how helping Emily would mean that he would achieve that goal. Other teachers had given him different activities to do. He cast his mind back to teachers talking about differentiated objectives and he remembered that his Science teacher had made this clear by putting objectives on the board for the class looking at gravity.

- All students are able to describe what is meant by gravity.
- Most students are able to apply this to an apple falling from a tree.
- Some students are able to explain how gravity differs depending on where you are in the galaxy.

Ravi remembered how he was encouraged to think about what would happen if he dropped an apple on the Moon rather than the Earth. The question had intrigued him and the teacher encouraged him to do some independent learning. He was set an extension task and used the books available in the lab to discover the answer.

As he reached the cafeteria Ravi felt calmer. Maybe he had been unfair to Emily, it was just that he was frustrated that the class couldn't move on to the next task until everyone had finished. Actually, he rather liked helping others and had come to realise that explaining things often helped him understand the topic rather more than he did when he was merely listening to the teacher.

Figure 11.2 Differentiation

Activity

Differentiation and stretching the most able are two of the biggest challenges for teachers. Think about how you could modify the lesson to ensure that Ravi was kept engaged. Things that you might like to think about could include how you:

- write your lesson plan to ensure that the most able are stretched;
- organise tasks to engage the most able without losing the rest of the class;
- talk to gifted and talented students about your intentions and what you would like them to do;
- use them to support less able students, without causing resentment.

Emily's story – supporting weaker students

Emily knew that she struggled in many of her classes. A turbulent home life as well as a lengthy illness meant that she had fallen behind her classmates at school and she always felt as though there were great chunks of her learning missing. She felt frustrated as she remembered her hopelessness as yet another teacher told her that she 'didn't understand how to use apostrophes', 'didn't understand the basics of long division' or 'couldn't structure paragraphs correctly'. She knew all of this – what she wanted was someone to fill in the gaps and actually show her how to do these things.

Normally Emily enjoyed working with Ravi. He was funny and smart and often explained things in a different way to the teacher and his way often helped her understand the topic. He would often explain something to her, leave her to it while he solved a more complicated problem and then come back to her to see how she was doing. This worked well but even he couldn't explain everything and today he seemed frustrated when the teacher had told the class that they would move to the next task when everyone had finished. The previous teacher had encouraged those that were struggling to come to an after-school club but that didn't seem to be happening at the moment.

The picture of the Van Gogh painting slipped out of her folder, holding it up, she began to forget about the lesson. The painting was magnificent, Emily wondered at the brushwork, she thought about the use of colour and started to contrast his use of texture with that of her other favourites, Manet, Monet and Cezanne. She wondered why not all had received the accolades she thought they deserved when they were alive and then began to wonder why the teacher had cut her off when she started talking enthusiastically about the painting. Why did she have to write down her thoughts when she preferred to talk?

Activity

Supporting students who are struggling in class can be a big challenge for teachers. If there are gaps in learning then it is often impossible to fill these gaps in a single lesson and other strategies need to be put in place. Looking back at the original lesson plan, think about strategies that you could put in place to support Emily.

Victor's story – being sensitive to religion and ethnicity

Victor always thought that growing up as the only non-white student in the small primary school he attended would mean that he became tough enough to ignore the actions of a minority of people who seemed intent on making digs at him. The reality was different and although he knew that he didn't always react in the right way, the frustration that built up inside him meant that occasionally even his strong faith, which preached tolerance and acceptance, was unable to hold him back from lashing out.

Most of the problems he faced stemmed from a lack of understanding by others. In the last year, he had been wished a happy Eid, good luck for Wesak and had been quizzed on Ramadan. None of which were relevant to his true religion. Victor tried to combat this ignorance by talking to people about his beliefs and asking everyone about their views but he found that many people found this a difficult conversation to have and, even when they did talk about the issues, it didn't always mean a change in attitude.

Victor appreciated the efforts many of his teachers took in ensuring that lessons embraced all cultures. He enjoyed the way in which literature from all over the world was used in his English classes and how the History lessons looked at major world events from different perspectives. He even appreciated the little touches in classes: not all people in case studies were given traditional English names and his favourite teachers asked him to talk to the class about any events affecting his religion. It wasn't always like that though and the incident in the Art class, where he had asked to go to the Prayer Room to pray for 20 minutes and had been refused, had upset him. He didn't know what to do about it, who to turn to, but he knew that he felt as though he should do something.

Reflection

To what extent should schools take into account individual ethnic and religious differences? Are there any practical steps schools can take to encourage tolerance and to support all students regardless of their origin? What should be the limit of these steps?

Marco's story – supporting students with special educational needs

At primary school, Marco always believed that he wasn't as intelligent as the other students. He struggled with his reading and always seemed to be the last to finish any written exercise that the teacher gave the class. He remembered how his Year 4 teacher would always interrupt when he was trying to read out loud and the impatient look on her face as she asked someone else to take over from Marco was etched in his memory and helped to confirm his personal view that he wasn't very bright.

His life changed when his form tutor in Year 7 encouraged him to go for a test for dyslexia. Marco would never forget the moment when he was told that his struggles were due to dyslexia rather than anything to do with his intelligence. Overnight he began to formulate strategies and slowly he began to work out what worked best for him. Changing the background colour of any documents to green helped focus the words as did changing fonts of documents. Teachers began to provide clearer documents for him, without any unnecessary detail and he found that illustrations helped him understand things better.

There were times when Marco felt as though he was back in Year 4, however, and today's Art class was one of those times. Being asked to read aloud was bad enough but when he was asked to come to the front of the room and write something on the board, Marco's heart had sunk. He knew that the teacher wasn't deliberately trying to embarrass him but he also knew that this was not the way that his needs would best be met which, as he rather tetchily muttered as he walked out of the room, the teacher would have known if they had bothered to talk to him.

Activity

Dyslexia is just one of a range of special educational needs that you might be asked to support within your classroom. For many there are clear strategies that can be adopted to help support the students, but the best advice is always to ask the students what works for them.

Select three of the special educational needs listed below and research strategies that might help you support students:

- Attention Deficit Hyperactivity Disorder (ADHD)
- Asperger Syndrome
- Autism
- Dyscalculia
- Dyspraxia
- Tourette's Syndrome

Figure 11.3 Coping with dyslexia

Mariam's story – engaging all students

As Mariam walked out of the classroom the usual emotions came to her. The amusement felt when Kasia repeated the English words that she had taught her, to the bafflement of the teacher, jostled with the guilt she felt as she dragged the lesson off at a tangent instead of looking at the Van Gogh picture. For the umpteenth time in her life, Mariam mentally kicked herself after she had gone for a cheap gag instead of concentrating on her work.

Although Mariam knew that she was bright, she was also aware that unless she focused on her work that potential would go to waste as she would not pass her exams. Often, she wondered why she had taken to the role of class clown with such panache. Thinking back to her childhood she remembered her mother telling her friends that 'Mariam is really good at making us laugh.' The words stuck with her and she resolved to continue to be good at this. Throughout her school career she had revelled in her ability to make others laugh and she knew that this talent made her popular with her classmates. What they didn't realise was that Mariam didn't always want to play this role. She felt pressure when something happened in the classroom and everyone turned to her to hear what she had to say, and in her more reflective moments she knew she wanted to step down from her role as a class clown but she wasn't sure how to do so.

Figure 11.4 The class clown

Activity

All your students will have different characters and the trick is to make best use of them in your class. You can't ask people to change their characters so instead think of ways of using students' characteristics to help the lesson.

Kasia's story – students with English as an additional language

England had been Kasia's home for the last two years and in general she enjoyed living here. She had made new friends, she liked the area that her family had settled in and, although she missed her own country, she was content. Back home she had always been in the top few students in her class and she had passed every exam that she had taken with flying colours.

The one problem she was having with settling into her new home was in gaining an understanding of the English language. She was trying hard but she still didn't understand everything that was going on in the class and had to rely on the support of Mariam and others. This meant that in some classes, as had happened in the Art class, she felt that she appeared to be less intelligent than the others in the group although she knew this was just her inability to express herself.

Figure 11.5 ESOL chicken

Feeling rather sorry for herself she reflected on the classes that went well for her. She felt happy when the teacher asked her what worked for her, and the Science teacher made a special effort to pronounce her name correctly and occasionally used a few examples from her home country. Her Geography teacher encouraged her to use an electronic translator to make sure that she understood the questions correctly and was always patient when waiting for answers as she struggled to put across her points in her second language. Smiling, she remembered how the teacher had used visual clues as well, slowing her speech down when Kasia was struggling to follow the principles of continental shelf formation. The memory helped to banish the memories of feeling lost and helpless in the Art class. Shaking her head, she resolved to talk to the teacher next time she didn't understand anything rather than rely on Mariam.

Reflection

With an increasing number of students for whom English is not their first language, the issue of literacy and its importance has become a key focus of assessment policy.

Think about the importance you attach to it. Would you mark down a student who has a superb grasp of concepts but for whom grammatical errors are common due to English not being their first language? Similarly, would you give extra marks to a student whose technical accuracy in English is exemplary even if the content of what they write is not strong?

Things to think about

These six case studies have been designed to get you thinking about the diverse needs of the typical class. Including everyone is always the goal and although meeting every single need might feel like an impossible task, there are a few things that you can do which would help all students. Talking to each person is key, so think about how you can best discuss the individual needs of students. Sharing good practice in the staffroom also gives you an insight into the strategies other people use. So can you think of mechanisms that will help you do that? Finally, learning from classes that don't go well helps you filter out what works and what doesn't work when trying to be an inclusive teacher. Is there a simple evaluation you can complete that will help you understand how the lesson went?

In a nutshell

This resource can be photocopied and used as a revision tool or a prompt for discussion with your peers. It is designed to help you think about how to become an inclusive teacher and what variables you can control.

Supporting students with dyslexia

Kirby *et al.* (2008) studied a group of students with dyslexia and concluded that many of the strategies that worked with students with dyslexia were also applicable to all students and so it was important not to 'single individual students out'.

The key finding was that every student was different and what works for one does not necessarily work for others, so knowing your students is crucial.

Often students with dyslexia have been told in the past that they are not very intelligent and so one of the key things a teacher can do is to help build their confidence and convince them of their ability.

Source: Kirby *et al.* (2008).

Putting it into practice

Select a handout that you use in your teaching and study it to see how 'dyslexic friendly' it is. Some of the common strategies used include:

- using sans serif fonts;
- experimenting with colour in writing and background;
- using illustrations rather than including too much text;
- using short sentences;
- making sure that the layout is clear and uncluttered;
- where possible using multisensory activities rather than just a handout;
- scaffolding learning to show the connections;
- providing handouts in advance so students can study them.

Once you have modified the handout, use it in a class and then ask students to evaluate it to see if they have any more ideas for improvement.

Suggestions for further reading

Wearmouth, J (2012) *Special Educational Needs: The Basics*. Abingdon: Routledge.

References

Kirby, J, Silvestri, R, Allingham, B, Parrila, R and La Fave, C (2008) 'Learning strategies and study approaches of postsecondary students with dyslexia', *Journal of Learning Disabilities*, 41 (1): 85–96.

Whyte, W (1952) 'Groupthink', *Fortune*, 45: 114–17.

12

How do we learn? How should we teach?

In this chapter we will explore:

- **how we learn;**
- **approaches to teaching;**
- **learning as transformation.**

Introduction

If you were asked to describe how you learn, what would you say? Would you make reference to how you have practised a skill or memorised information for a test, or perhaps you might cite ways in which your ideas have changed and how this has influenced your life. Learning can be difficult to define – there is a variety of dictionary definitions which relate to the acquisition of knowledge and skills through to changes in behaviour, and others which suggest that learning has more in common with the development of an open mind. In this chapter we will explore theories relating to learning and use these as a basis to consider approaches to teaching. You will be encouraged to think about a variety of approaches to allow for greater flexibility and help you to generate your own ideas about teaching.

What is learning?

The definitions of learning provided in the introduction show learning as a broad concept, influenced by both psychology and environment. Many definitions refer to changes in behaviour which, it could be argued, suggest that learning has much in common with 'conditioning' (thereby placing the control for learning outside the individual), so an alternative definition could be . . . *any process that in living organisms leads to permanent capacity change and which is not solely due to biological maturation or ageing* (Illeris, 2007: 3). Learning might also be considered perspective transformation in that it opens up new thoughts, ideas and possibilities. According to Mezirow transformative learning is . . . *a process by which we transform problematic frames of reference (mindsets, habits of mind, meaning perspectives) – sets of assumption and expectation – to make them more inclusive, discriminating, open, reflective and emotionally able to change* (Mezirow, in Illeris, 2009: 92).

The broad definitions of learning are not helpful to teachers in terms of supporting you to plan and structure your lessons and to assist in the construction of learning objectives which are meaningful as they simply provide an overview. What is more important is to develop your own understanding which will guide your approach.

Reflection

Using your education and current learning as a basis, try to develop your own definition of learning. If you are keeping a reflective log, this is something you could add to it.

Having a clear and meaningful understanding of learning is not an easy task and many definitions can be critically analysed in relation to your own experiences as a student and as a teacher. Our definition of learning is based on our values as teachers, alongside our experiences as perpetual students:

> *Learning is remembering, using and evaluating knowledge and skills to enable changes in perspective and behaviour.*

Enabling learning is, of course, central to the teacher's role and exploring various theories related to learning will provide you with a basis from which to reflect on the best way to structure your teaching.

Categories of learning

As outlined in Chapter 9, Bloom (1956) set out to categorise learning into three domains each with corresponding 'levels' of learning. You have already been introduced to those set out for the cognitive domain; in addition to this, learning objectives linked to the psychomotor and affective development were developed.

The psychomotor domain relates to the physical activities usually associated with skills development and considers movement and associated mental processes; for example, learning to ride a bicycle requires mastery of some physical skills as well as thinking through the process of actions. Simpson (1972) produced a 'ladder' of learning relating to skills which is outlined in Table 12.1. The lowest-level skills are shown on the first row, so, according to the theory, learning in this domain starts with perception and moves up the ladder until it reaches origination.

Table 12.1 Levels of learning: psychomotor domain

Perception: Using sensory cues to guide activity.	For example - estimates where a ball will land after it has been thrown in order to catch.
Set: Being ready to act (think ready, set ... go). This is also referred to as 'mindset'.	For example - knows and acts upon a sequence of steps in a process.
Guided response: Imitation and trial and error.	For example - performs a task following a demonstration.
Mechanism: Learned responses have become habitual and can be performed with confidence.	For example - being able to change gear on a car when required.
Complex overt response: Skilful performance of complex movements.	For example - able to dance numerous steps in the waltz in time with the music.
Adaptation: Skills are well developed and can be modified to suit the individual.	For example - responds effectively to unexpected events (without mishap).
Origination: Creating new movement patterns to fit a particular situation.	For example - develops a new dance.

The affective domain is concerned with emotions and has also been presented as a hierarchy to illustrate the various levels of associated 'skill' (Krathwohl *et al.*, 1964) (see Figure 12.1 and Table 12.2).

Figure 12.1 Affective learning

Table 12.2 Levels of learning: affective domain

Receiving - Sensing external stimuli, awareness and selected attention.	For example - feeling/capturing an experience.
Responding - Actively attending and responding to stimuli.	For example - active listening and contributing to a conversation.
Valuing - Acceptance or commitment to a value.	For example - sharing your beliefs and valuing different perspectives.
Organisation - Conceptualisation of values/ organisation of a value system.	For example - recognising the need for balance to accommodate beliefs.
Characterisation - Internalisation of values.	For example - works according to own values/ethics and values others for who they are.

Cognitivist approaches to learning

Cognitivism is concerned with how we understand information rather than how we react to it (behaviourism), so a number of learning theories fit into this category. A cognitivist approach has a focus on processes such as thinking and problem-solving and cognitivist theorists such as Bruner, Piaget and Ausubel wanted to discover how information was received, organised and stored. In this sense, cognitivism is based on an information processing model with the human brain being compared to a computer. In its simplest form, this would mean that teaching would focus on 'programming' by developing strategies which would allow relevant information to be structured and retained. However, it is also important to remember that humans are much more complex than computers and can interact with information in the same way as they interact with the environment, and as a result develop different mental representations from the same set of information. An important consideration therefore for teaching is the ways in which learners are involved in the learning process.

The role of structure in learning would be central to a cognitivist approach and, according to Bruner, when new learning is introduced, it should be done so in relation to things previously encountered. This notion underpins the idea of a 'spiral curriculum' that, as it develops, revisits basic ideas frequently, building upon them until students have fully grasped the subjects (Bruner, 1977). According to cognitivist theorists we process information based on how we have learnt to cognise and make connections by linking new information with old. Ausubel referred to this as meaningful learning (as opposed to rote learning) and suggested that learning could be improved by the introduction of 'advance organisers'. An advance organiser is information that is presented prior to learning to help the learner organise the new information, for example the use of a concept map or telling a story which puts the learning into context (Ausubel, 1960),

Piaget is best known for his work on stages of development which provided an outline of cognitive development according to age. There are four stages in this model and each stage involves the acquisition of new skills which is dependent upon the successful completion of the preceding stage.

Sensorimotor 0–2 years

Until about four months of age an infant cannot distinguish people from objects but gradually learns to do so. At this stage children learn by touching objects and physically exploring the environment.

Pre-operational 2–7 years

During this stage children acquire a mastery of a language and are able to use words to represent objects and images. At this stage children remain egocentric and interpret the world from their own position.

Concrete operation period 7–11 years

At this stage children are much less egocentric and master abstract, logical notions. They are able to handle ideas such as cause and effect and can carry out mathematical calculations.

Formal operation period 11+ years

During adolescence, the developing child becomes more able to comprehend abstract and hypothetical concepts. When faced with a problem they should be able to review all possible ways of solving it and go through them systematically.

Constructivism

Another branch of cognitivism is constructivism which understands learning as an active process in which learners construct their own representations of knowledge. It differs from the cognitivist approach in that it considers knowledge to be something which is uniquely constructed by individuals rather than something external which can be passed on to a learner. There are some similarities to epistemology (outlined in Chapter 1) in that our experiences have an influence on the ways in which we construct meaning. Learning is therefore seen as an active process through which learners use sensory input to construct meaning and is based on the premise that learning is not simply about the passive acceptance of conventional 'knowledge' but an active process in which learners engage with the world. Most cognitivists would assume there is a 'real world' from which we learn, whereas constructivists believe that the mind produces its own unique reality, therefore we create meaning rather than acquire it (Jonassen, 1991).

Gestalt

As with other cognitivist approaches, 'gestalt' is concerned with how we perceive, organise and structure information in the learning process. The translation of the word relates to patterns and shape and the theory is based on the human tendency to give form to parts of information in order to create meaning. Descriptions of gestalt learning theory often refer to the whole, in that the whole is seen is greater than the sum of its parts, an assumption which suggests that if we see the big picture we will have an understanding of how the picture evolved. It may be more correct to approach the theory from the perspective that the whole differs from the parts – in this way learners would be encouraged to discover the underlying nature of a topic or problem and consider the relationship between the various elements.

Gestalt theory is often illustrated using images to show how, when we are given selected parts of information, the brain completes the gaps and perceives a whole. This can be illustrated by

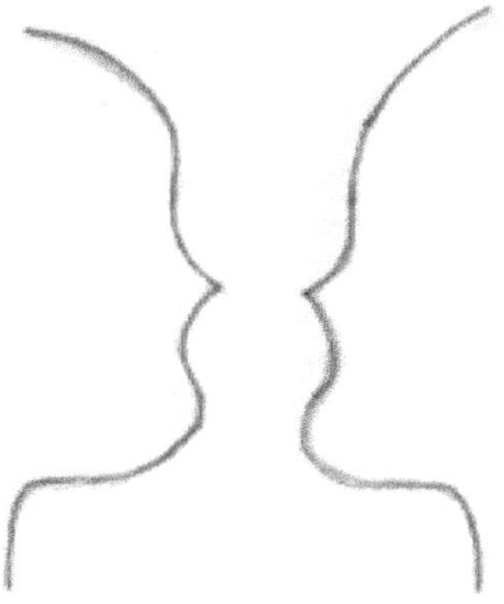

Figure 12.2 Gestalt

Figure 12.2 In this image what do you see? Is it a vase or two faces? In fact, it is simply lines on a page but this represents the mental tendency to organise perceptions so that they 'make sense'.

Gestalt as applied to learning theory is based on the organisation of information which gives importance to structure and how various parts of a subject fit together. Based on this premise gaps and inconsistencies are considered important stimuli for learning and, as a result, learning becomes a form of problem-solving. The main goal of the theory is to encourage the brain to view the parts as well as the sum of the parts, therefore teachers should encourage students to discover relationships between the various elements of a topic.

Behaviourist approaches to learning

Behaviourism is based on the hypothesis that behaviour is a response to external events and can be explained without giving consideration to internal processes such as mental activities – in a sense it is a form of reflex learning. The focus is on the changes in observable behaviours, therefore we would assume learning had taken place if the desired behaviours were presented to us.

Pavlov's (1927) experiments related to classical conditioning are typical examples of this. These experiments were intended to show how a dog could be taught to respond in a particular way to a given stimulus. The initial stimulus (food) produced an unconditioned response in the dog (saliva). Pavlov then presented the stimulus together with what he referred to as a 'conditioned stimulus' (a bell) in order to teach the dog that he would be rewarded with food when the bell rang. Eventually the dog learned to respond by salivating at the sound of the bell, so the conditioned stimulus then produced a conditioned response.

Similar studies were extended to humans in the 1920s, the most famous of these being the 'Little Albert Experiments' carried out by Watson and Raynor. Watson claimed that psychology was not concerned with the mind or human consciousness but only with behaviour, therefore man could be studied objectively like other animals. Little Albert was a nine-month-old baby who was studied to test his reactions to various stimuli. These included a white rabbit, a monkey, a rat and various masks.

Figure 12.3 Little Albert

Albert showed no fear of any of these stimuli. However, what did shock and then scare him was the sound of a hammer being struck against a steel bar close to his head. This would cause Albert to cry and try to crawl away. When little Albert was 11 months old the white rat was presented to him accompanied by the hammer being struck against the steel bar. This was done several times until eventually Albert would only have to see the rat before he burst into tears. Later, little Albert generalised these events to a fear of things which were similar.

The classic conditioning experiments describe a common-sense experience of learning by association and were extended by Skinner (1948) to emphasise the importance of positive and negative reinforcement. Positive reinforcement occurs when some expression of approval is made to a person when a desired behaviour is observed and negative reinforcement when something is removed to indicate that the desired behaviour is not present. According to Skinner, behaviour which is reinforced tends to be repeated or strengthened and behaviour which is not reinforced tends to die out. The process was described as operant conditioning. Anyone who has trained a dog to follow simple commands such as 'sit' or 'shake a paw' will be familiar with the way in which positive reinforcement can be used to condition certain responses.

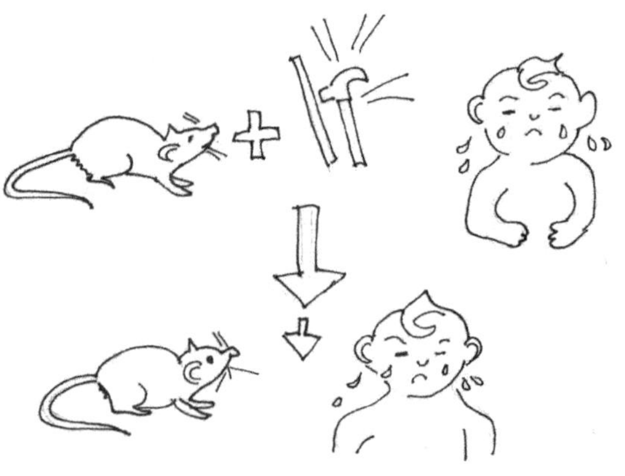

Figure 12.4 Reinforcement in action

Activity

In which ways is positive and negative reinforcement used in the classroom? Compile a list of strategies used to reinforce positive behaviours and those used to reduce less desirable behaviours.

Social learning theory

Social learning theory is based on the premise that we learn from each other and that social interaction plays a fundamental role in our development. According to Bandura (1977), as children we observe the people around us and through this learn to behave in certain ways. This process is known as modelling and was illustrated during Bandura's Bobo doll experiments which were set up to investigate how certain behaviours (in this case aggression) can be learnt through observation and imitation. In this experiment, the children who observed adult models acting aggressively towards a Bobo doll imitated this behaviour when left alone with the doll. According to Bandura: *Most human behaviour is learned observationally through modelling: from observing others one forms an idea of how new behaviours are performed and on later occasions this coded information serves as a guide for action* (Bandura, 1977: 22).

Figure 12.5 Modelling

This theory can be extended to the classroom to show the influence of 'significant' others, such as teachers and peers, in the learning context and as a result show how the learning environment will affect how we think and what we think about.

Activity

Read through the following excerpt from a reflective journal. Using what you know about social learning theory, write down a few points on what you think went wrong.

> *Today's class was about ordering lunch in a restaurant. The students really seemed to like the way the room had been set up as restaurant tables and the fact that they could take turns in being served or taking food orders. They absolutely loved the menus and seemed to have fun with attempting pronunciation of some of the more tricky words ... Ewa really seemed to struggle with the word 'lapin' ... which sounded more like lappin. Very funny really and most of the group were laughing and making fun of her accent. She seemed to enjoy the attention when Jamie started to immitate her, I even laughed ... but then, everyone else in the class did the same thing and I noticed that Ewa seemed to get a little stressed ... I don't know what happened but by the time we got to the plenary the whole class was out of control.*

Humanist approaches to learning

According to humanist theories, learning is a natural desire and an attempt to reach our full potential. As a result, learning is focused on the process rather than the outcome. This approach was advocated by Rudolf Steiner, who believed that education should be designed to meet the changing needs of a child as they develop and that children should not be pushed towards society's goals.

A central premise of the humanist approach is encouraging learner autonomy, therefore learners should have more control over the learning process. The teacher, rather than being the wise sage, would become the facilitator who acts as a role model and encourages all learners to contribute to lessons. According to Rogers, learning should be student-centred and the conditions in which learning takes place are the key to learners' development. The conditions referred to included 'realness', 'acceptance', 'empathic understanding' (Rogers, 1983).

A humanistic approach to teaching would have an emphasis on the active search for meaning and the fulfilment of individual goals rather than teachers being the purveyors of knowledge and professors of what should be learnt. It would be based on the assumption that motivation towards learning comes from within.

Learning as transformation

At the beginning of this chapter we attempted to define learning by making reference to our own and others' definition of what it means to learn. Within those definitions reference was made to learning as a change of perspective, a process which has been described as 'transformational'. As described in Chapter 6, according to Mezirow, we all have certain 'frames of reference' based on our experiences, associations and conditioned responses and these frames shape the ways in which we understand new experiences. This has a very useful function in providing structure and helping generate understanding of new learning, but frames may also be limiting as they will tend to lead to habitual understandings of new experiences. By becoming critically aware of our assumptions and perceptions we are in a better position . . . *to extend our understanding and make alternative choices* (Mezirow, 1997: 167).

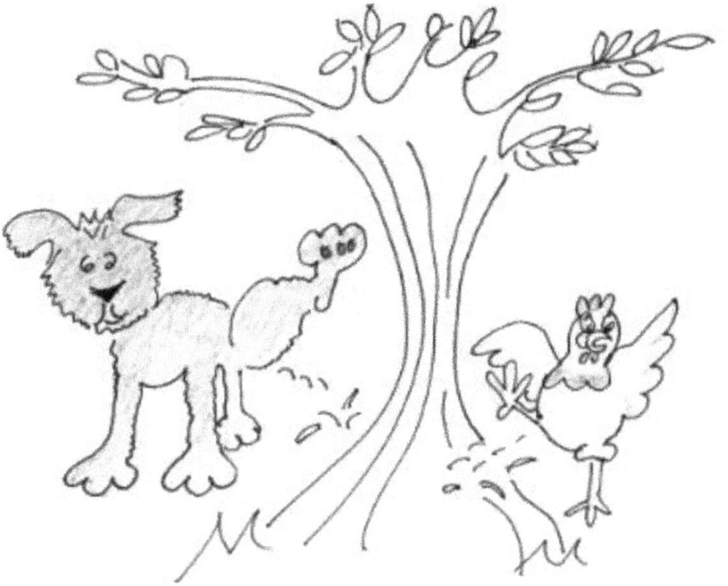

Figure 12.6 Frames of reference

Although many of the theories outlined in this chapter are quite old, they are still relevant to today's classroom and underpin much of classical psychology. That said, it is important to remember that it is difficult to establish a theory beyond all doubt and for this reason it is important to spend time thinking about your personal approach to teaching and learning, taking into account your own students. This will provide the basis from which you can reflect and work out the best approaches for your classroom, your learners, your organisation and yourself.

A note about teaching

There are many powerful images of 'expert teachers' which might lead us to think that teaching is the domain of the most charismatic and dedicated among us. Consider popular films such as *Dead Poets Society* or *Dangerous Minds* and you will be presented with an image of individuals who motivate and inspire on a daily basis. While this may be a very admirable aspiration, it is also worth remembering that learners respond to many different types of teachers and teaching is simply about helping people to learn: *The point of teaching is to help someone acquire information, develop skills, generate insights and internalise dispositions they did not know before* (Brookfield, 2013: 9).

Things to think about

Learning theories provide a conceptual framework and ideas about how knowledge is absorbed, structured and processed during learning but they do not provide all the answers. There are other factors such as cognitive, emotional and environmental influences to consider. In what ways can you use a knowledge of learning theory to help develop your practice? What new insights will help you in planning future learning experiences?

In a nutshell

This feature covers the essentials of learning theories to provide some examples of how these can be used to inform your practice. This resource can be photocopied and used as a revision tool or a prompt for discussion with your peers.

Learning theories	Putting it into practice
Cognitivism – We develop mental or visual representations of events and create meaning from this information. Information is processed on how we learn to cognise and make connections. The emphasis is on structure, organisation and patterns.	**Cognitivist approaches** – provide opportunities for students to create their own meaning through active approaches such as games and practical activities. Use concept maps and graphical organisers to display key points
Gestalt – We perceive selected parts of information and tend to create 'wholes'. Learning is about problem-solving through understanding the function of various parts and how they fit together.	**Gestalt** – create opportunities for learners to explore and have insights into the connections between the parts and whole topics. Use experiments, concept maps and jigsaws.
Humanism – learning is a natural process and learners should be encouraged to be autonomous. The teacher is the facilitator of an active search for learning and supports individual development.	**Humanism** – create opportunities for individual learning through differentiated approaches and student-centred activities. Use individual learning plans to set targets and track progress.
Behaviourism – based on principles of classical and operant conditioning. Learning is seen as a response to experiences and the use of positive and negative reinforcement is effective in helping us to learn. We learn from what we experience frequently, leading to behaviour changes.	**Behaviourism** – use learning checks and short activities in order to revisit and reinforce learning. Provide opportunities for experiential learning.
Social learning theory – emphasises the importance of learning with and from others. Modelling describes how we learn by observing and imitating influential others.	**Social learning theory** – create opportunities for individuals to learn from each other. Use group work and peer teaching and assessment. Activities such as debates and discussion are effective.

Suggestions for further reading

Illeris, K (ed.) (2009) *Contemporary Theories of Learning, Learning Theorists . . . in Their Own Words*. Oxford: Routledge.

References

Ausubel, DP (1960) 'The use of advance organizers in the learning and retention of meaningful verbal material', *Journal of Educational Psychology*, 51: 267–72.

Bandura, A (1977) *Social Learning Theory*. Englewood Cliffs, NJ: Prentice Hall.

Bloom, BS (1956) *A Taxonomy of Educational Objectives: The Classification of Educational Goals, Handbook 1: Cognitive Domain*. Ann Arbor, MI: Longman Green.

Brookfield, S (2013) *Powerful Techniques for Teaching in Lifelong Learning*. Maidenhead: Open University Press.

Bruner, J (1977) *The Process of Education: A Landmark in Educational Theory*. Cambridge, MA: Harvard University Press.

Illeris, K (2007) *How We Learn: Learning and Non-learning in School and Beyond*. London and New York: Routledge.

Jonassen, DH (1991) 'Evaluating constructivistic learning', *Educational Technology*, 31 (9): 28–33.

Krathwohl, DR, Bloom, BS and Masia, BB (1964) *Taxonomy of Educational Objectives, Book II. Affective Domain*. New York: David McKay.

Mezirow, J (1997) *Transformative Dimensions of Adult Learning*. San Francisco, CA: Jossey-Bass.

Pavlov, IP (1927*) Conditioned Reflexes: An Investigation of the Physiological Activity of the Cerebral Cortex*, trans. GV Anrep. London: Oxford University Press.

Rogers, CR (1983) *Freedom to Learn for the 80's*. New York: Charles E. Merrill.

Simpson, EJ (1972) *The Classification of Educational Objectives in the Psychomotor Domain*. Washington, DC: Gryphon House.

Skinner, BF (1948) '"Superstition" in the pigeon', *Journal of Experimental Psychology*, 38: 168–72.

Watson, JB and Rayner, R (1920) 'Conditioned emotional reactions', *Journal of Experimental Psychology*, 3 (1): 1–14.

13

Creating a positive classroom

In this chapter we will explore:

- **factors impacting on classroom environment;**
- **how to establish a safe learning environment;**
- **modelling positive attitudes, values and behaviours.**

Introduction

When you think about a 'positive classroom' your thoughts might initially be drawn to environmental factors such as the shape and size of the room, the layout of the desks, whether or not the walls are adorned with colourful posters and learners' work. These are important factors but possibly not the most important. If you were to spend every day of your life in an environment which made you feel uncomfortable, what impact would that have? What if you felt as if you didn't belong, were being ignored or just couldn't participate . . . is that something which would influence your ability to learn? The answer is obvious of course. The classroom environment is a key component of teaching and learning; it is a place in which all learners should feel valued and safe. Learning should not be about simply absorbing information, it should be a process in which we develop a range of skills and knowledge and it is part of the teaching role to ensure that the classroom is a positive place which respects individuals, demonstrates cultural sensitivity and encourages each individual to develop their abilities.

Factors impacting on the classroom environment

I never teach my pupils, I only attempt to provide the conditions in which they can learn is a famous quote from Einstein. Although the original may well have been referring to a humanistic approach to teaching and learning, in a literal sense this is also important. It is every teacher's responsibility to ensure that the classroom is a safe and stimulating environment which has the potential to create positive learning experiences. When we start teaching it is very easy to focus on the content of

Figure 13.1 Super teacher

lessons; we want to be sure that we are teaching the right things in the right way and that we are helping our students to achieve their aims in terms of assessment outcomes. This is all important of course but is it more – or less – important than the classroom environment?

Illeris (2009) suggests that all learning comprises three different dimensions:

- **The content dimension** – relating to what is learnt. In subject specifications, this is often described as knowledge and skills but in a wider sense could also include things like attitudes and behaviours.
- **The incentive dimension** – which directs mental energy to the learning process and includes feelings, emotions and motivation towards learning.
- **The interaction dimension** – which could be described as the 'social' element as it initiates the learning process, including the transmission of information.

Therefore every single learning process is 'stretched' out between three angles or approaches, each having an impact on the learning process.

If the aim of learners is to develop an understanding of the subject, then their initial focus is likely to be on the cognitive content. However, how the particular lesson is experienced by the individual (the emotions and motivations attached to the process) will have a big influence on how it may be remembered. Alongside this the social interaction – the student interaction (or student–teacher interaction) – will also impact on how learning is remembered. It is possible that while appropriate

Figure 13.2 The three dimensions of learning

Adapted from Illeris (2009).

strategies may have helped to present new learning in an interesting and informative way, psychological and interactional aspects of a lesson can affect the meaning of this content so that learning has been distorted, has not taken place at all or that something completely different has been learnt, for example a dislike of the subject or negative impression of the teacher.

Reflective task

During an Art lesson, the teacher is explaining the use of light and shade and then asks the students to create a pencil drawing using shading to indicate shape and depth. The students are then put into pairs so that they can critique each other's work. Mishti, a normally quiet and shy girl, seems really animated about this activity and is very pleased with the drawing she has produced. She has used shading very effectively even if the picture is quite difficult to decipher. As she proudly holds her picture up, her partner Tom laughs and starts making jokes, completely forgetting to say what had been done well. Mishti starts to cry and runs out of the room.

In this example what do you think Mishti will remember from that class? Will her focus be on the main objective and how she had managed to use light and shade in her drawing? Or is it possible that she has come away with a very different message, for example, 'I can't draw . . . I hate art . . .' Clearly there are things the teacher could have done differently to ensure that learning in the lesson was the intended learning by focusing on all elements of the classroom environment.

Establishing a safe learning environment

Classroom environment is a key factor in how students will feel about learning and there are a number of things that teachers can take charge of in relation to this. These could be grouped as the practical and social aspects of the classroom.

Practical aspects

Consider the layout of the room and how you want to use the space. If you intend to use lots of group work, then desks and chairs need to be organised in groupings that allow students to interact easily. If you intend to present information from the front of the room and then get students to work in groups then ensure it is easy to move chairs around so that the different activities of listening and discussion can be used. Some typical classroom layouts include the horseshoe or a square where students sit on three sides, which is useful when you want students to be able to listen, take notes and get involved in whole-group discussion. It allows the students to see you and each other and for you to see all of them. There may be times when you don't want students to take notes and would like them to focus on a group discussion, in which case you could remove desks to the sides of the room and have a circle of chairs. Alternatively you could have nested tables and chairs in small groups which are very effective for small-group work.

Figure 13.3 Nested tables

Another practical consideration relates to the aesthetics of the room. It is important to try to create as pleasant an environment as possible. This can be done by giving thought to the wall displays and the use of colour. Displaying student work can be an effective way of making the students feel at home but you also need to consider how you organise this. It is also important to remember to change displays so that you don't have the same work (from the same people) displayed at all times.

Social aspects

As outlined in Chapter 12, social aspects of learning have a big impact on our development. According to Vygotsky (1978), we learn first at a social level (interpersonal) and later at an individual level (intrapersonal). As humans, it is natural for us to want to make sense of the world and often this learning is the result of social interaction – just think how often a young child asks questions about everything and then starts to formulate their own meaning from the answers. Vygotsky (1978) suggested that the teacher's role should be one of guidance and highlighted the importance of recognising the Zone of Proximal Development (ZPD) which means recognising the difference between what a learner can do without help and what has not yet been learnt (outlined in Chapter 10). The zone of proximal development has become synonymous with the term *scaffolding* outlined by Wood *et al.* (1976) to refer to the support put in place to fill the gap between current and future learning. To encourage autonomy and higher-level thinking, when the learner has mastered a particular task, the scaffolding should be removed. Vygotsky also viewed interaction between learners as being an effective way of developing skills and learning strategies and was an advocate of cooperative learning techniques.

Activity

Make a list of all the strategies you use (or could use) which you would describe as collaborative learning. Talk this through with your mentor and plan an activity including one of these strategies.

Rules and respect

A positive classroom is one which is based on respect; this means respect for the teacher, respect from the teacher and respect for everyone in the group. This can, and should, be extended beyond the classroom, in that a positive classroom is one which engenders respect for the wider community, acknowledges and accepts difference, and values diversity.

British values

Most teachers will be aware of the government's requirement to promote British values but may not be entirely clear on what that means. After all, we have lived in a multicultural society for many years and what we perceive as 'values' may well have changed, together with the diversity of the population. However, there is no need to be concerned about this – what the government defines as 'fundamental British Values' may just as easily be considered common values within democratic societies and are probably the values you would ordinarily convey within your teaching. These are:

- democracy;
- the rule of law;
- individual liberty.

According to Ofsted, schools and colleges should:

- enable students to distinguish right from wrong and to respect the civil and criminal law of England;
- encourage students to accept responsibility for their behaviour, show initiative and understand how they can contribute positively to the lives of those living and working in the locality of the school and to society more widely;
- enable students to acquire a broad general knowledge of and respect for public institutions and services in England;
- further tolerance and harmony between different cultural traditions by enabling students to acquire an appreciation of and respect for their own and other cultures;

- encourage respect for other people; and
- encourage respect for democracy and support for participation in the democratic processes, including respect for the basis on which the law is made and applied in England (Department for Education, 2014).

The creation of beliefs and values is not something which can simply be taught in a one-off lesson, so some thought should be given to how their ongoing development might be embedded into your teaching. Some simple ideas might be:

- develop discussion tasks which encourage the exploration of different cultures;
- celebrate a range of religious festivals;
- use research-based tasks to explore key principles;
- encourage a collaborative approach;
- confront bigotry and encourage open discussion;
- explore all sides of topical issues;
- challenge inappropriate language and behaviours;
- acknowledge teamworking, responsibility and initiative.

There is a range of activities you could incorporate but perhaps the key to success in this area is the genuine embedding of this type of activity in day-to-day teaching. This has the effect of 'normalising' the topics and encourages an open environment conducive to discussion when the opportunity arises.

Multiple intelligences

A key principle of generating a culture of mutual respect is in recognising the many ways in which individuals differ. As well as acknowledging the differences in culture, religion and race, we also need to be aware of the differences in abilities and skills, ensuring that every learner has the opportunity to develop and that we value abilities beyond those which lead to academic success. The theory of multiple intelligences was developed by Howard Gardner in 1983 and suggests that traditional notions of intelligence (based on IQ testing) are quite limited and limiting. As an alternative Gardner proposed that there were in fact eight types of intelligence which indicated the range of human abilities. These intelligences are:

- **Linguistic intelligence** – everything to do with language, speech, reading and writing.
- **Logical-mathematical intelligence** – the ability to work well with abstracts, science and logic.
- **Spatial intelligence** – the capacity to perceive the visual world accurately and to transform, modify and recreate aspects of one's visual world.
- **Bodily-kinaesthetic intelligence** – the ability to think in movement, being skilled in using the body, for example a dancer or a juggler.

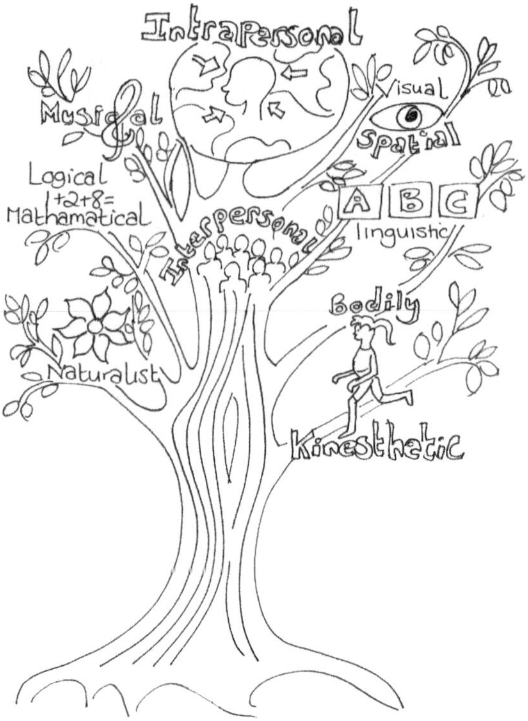

Figure 13.4 Gardner's tree

- **Musical intelligence** – the ability to think in sound, to hear without auditory stimuli, to be able to manipulate and combine elements of music without necessarily expressing them on a musical instrument.
- **Interpersonal intelligence** – the capacity to notice and make distinctions among other individuals, how you relate to others.
- **Intrapersonal intelligence** – the knowledge of self, the ability to draw upon your own feelings to guide your own behaviour.
- **Naturalist intelligence** – relates to an appreciation of the natural world as demonstrated by skilled botanists or gardeners.

Some later versions of the theory include a ninth intelligence referred to as 'existential intelligence' which relates to those with the ability to conceptualise larger questions about human existence.

Gardner's theory was not intended as a way of categorising individuals, nor a suggestion that individuals will only learn in one way, but a way of demonstrating that human potential goes beyond what was traditionally recognised by IQ tests. It is interesting from the perspective of acknowledging different abilities but is also helpful for teachers in identifying potential routes to learning when the more traditional logical approaches to instruction do not seem to be working. For example, if you were trying to teach the law of diminishing returns (continual increase in effort does not necessarily lead to increase in output) you could explain it and get students to read about it (verbal/linguistic), you could ask students to work out formulae (logical-mathematical) and create charts/graphs (spatial), they could create a song to explain the concept (musical), demonstrate the concept through movement (bodily-kinaesthetic), carry out a role play based on a case study showing the impact on a business (interpersonal) . . . and so on. This would take into account several of the multiple intelligences outlined in the theory, provide different routes to understanding the concept as well as opportunities for useful repetition – although we probably wouldn't suggest every strategy in one lesson!

Modelling positive attitudes, values and behaviours

As outlined in Chapter 12, social learning theory introduces the concept of modelling as a way in which we learn from others. Modelling is an effective strategy for encouraging desired behaviours as it provides an immediate 'template' for learners to follow. In a sense, teaching modelling is about practising what we preach: if we expect learners to follow rules then we must also show that we respect the rules; if we expect learners to show respect to each other, then we must also show respect to each of them.

Modelling may take many forms, in that we may model our beliefs and values through open discussion and through our responses to questions. We can model our approach to completing tasks by ensuring that we complete the things we say we will complete by the deadline that was provided. Modelling is also demonstrated through our use of language and our overall demeanour.

As outlined in Chapter 6, the NLP pre-supposition 'You cannot not communicate' suggests that at all times we are modelling because every behaviour is a form of communication. This is based on the work of Watzlawick *et al.* (1967) outlining the basic maxims of communication.

Reflective task

Think about your ideal classroom environment. What behaviours would the teacher be modelling? How might they look, how would they interact with students? Now reflect on your own teaching - go back through your reflective journal if you are keeping one. What attitudes and behaviours have you modelled?

A note of caution

Based on the content of this chapter, it would be easy to assume that good teaching simply means a positive approach to both teaching and learning. While this certainly helps it is also worth considering the bigger picture which is that, whatever approach we take to teaching, the focus must be on creating the conditions in which real learning can take place. Creating a positive culture is not simply a matter of being positive – there will be times when we need to correct misconceptions, challenge behaviours and acknowledge that things could be improved. Being positive does not mean treating our learners as if they are delicate beings who cannot accept criticism or corrective feedback, nor is it about simply acknowledging the good and disregarding the rest. A positive learning environment is one in which both teachers and learners can explore new territory together and in which there is acceptance that there will be successes as well as failures.

As well as being a positive experience and fun, learning is also hard work and according to Atherton (2013 online) this should be recognised: *It is hard work. It does not have to be miserable work, but any denial of the work aspect inevitably compromises standards.* On that basis, we can create a positive learning environment by honest communication, clarity in expectations and acknowledging that learning can and should be challenging.

Things to think about

There are a number of factors which have a positive or negative effect on the classroom environment and it is important to consider the social and emotional factors alongside the content of lessons. What factors impact on your classroom environment? Does recognition of these factors allow you to manage negative impacts and maximise the impact of the positive?

In a nutshell

This feature covers the dimensions of learning and provides some examples of how this theory can be used to inform your practice. This resource can be photocopied and used as a revision tool or a prompt for discussion with your peers.

The dimensions of learning

Illeris (2009) suggests that all learning comprises three different dimensions:

- Learning has a content of skill or meaning.
- Learning is an emotional process that requires incentive.
- Learning is a social process and involves interaction.

Therefore, every single learning process is 'stretched' out between three angles.

Source: Illeris (2009).

Putting it into practice

For students the immediate focus is usually on the cognitive element. However, how the particular lesson is experienced by the individual will have a big influence on how it may be remembered.

When planning take into account content and incentive and include opportunities for interaction with the lesson content and with other learners.

- Create a supportive classroom.
- Generate a culture of collaboration.
- Check that (intended) learning is taking place.
- Plan well BUT adapt plans.
- Differentiate activities.
- Take opportunities to encourage discussion around key topics.
- Model positive behaviours.
- Set clear expectations.
- Use Socratic questioning to develop higher-level thinking.

Suggestions for further reading

Illeris, K (ed.) (2009) *Contemporary Theories of Learning: Learning Theorists . . . in Their Own Words.* Oxford: Routledge

References

Atherton, JS (2013) *Doceo: Against a Positive Learning Environment* (online UK), retrieved 22 May 2017 from **http://doceo.co.uk/heterodoxy/positive.htm**

Department for Education (2014) *Promoting Fundamental British Values as Part of SMSC in Schools.* London: Crown.

Gardner, H (1983) *Frames of Mind: The Theory of Multiple Intelligences.* New York: Basic Books.

Rosenthal, R and Jacobson, L (1992) *Pygmalion in the Classroom,* expanded edition. New York: Irvington.

Vygotsky, LS (1978) *Mind in Society.* Cambridge, MA: Harvard University Press.

Watzlawick, P, Beavin-Bavelas, J and Jackson, D (1967) 'Some tentative axioms of communication', in *Pragmatics of Human Communication – A Study of Interactional Patterns, Pathologies and Paradoxes.* New York: W.W. Norton.

Wood, D, Bruner, J and Ross, G (1976) 'The role of tutoring in problem solving', *Journal of Child Psychology and Child Psychiatry,* 17: 89–100.

14

Effective classroom management

In this chapter we will explore:

- **factors affecting behaviour;**
- **behaviour management strategies;**
- **the impact of communication.**

Introduction

Figure 14.1 Chaos in the classroom

When starting their career, many new teachers have the issue of behaviour management at the forefront of their mind. Many worry that 'they won't do what I tell them to do' and although this fades in time effective classroom management is still an important aspect of a teacher's job. At the heart of effective classroom management is the need for clear communication and the avoidance of any misunderstandings (either deliberate or otherwise) by students. This chapter will build on how to maintain a positive classroom and identify how you ensure that students stay on track in class and how to ensure that your stress levels stay low!

Factors affecting behaviour

Reflection

Picture the scene. You have asked your Year 10 students to complete a series of questions based on a scene in *Romeo and Juliet*. The majority of the class start the task immediately but one student, Etienne, appears not to be working at all and, to make matters worse, the fact that he is not working is unsettling those around him.

What would you do in this situation?

The obvious answer is to go over and tell Etienne to start work but is this enough? If we verbally tell the student to get on with their work are we missing any underlying issues? Think about the possible reasons why Etienne is not working.

- He doesn't understand the questions.
- He is being distracted by things going on outside the classroom.
- He is missing something he needs to answer the questions.
- He is being distracted by someone/something.
- He is deliberately avoiding doing the tasks.

Although this is not an exhaustive list, it is indicative of many of the reasons why students fail to participate in class. Now, if you take a direct approach, then the only point you are really addressing is the last one – the others will still be present when you walk away. To ensure that all reasons are addressed, maintaining open lines of communication is vital. This will help you understand why a student is not doing what they should be doing.

Communicating in class

Wilbur Schramm's model of communication helps us understand the dynamics that exist within the classroom. Schramm (1954) talked about the problems of communicating and how the message can get lost if you are not careful. The major problem when communicating is what Schramm

Figure 14.2 An interesting topic . . .

called 'noise'. This comprises anything that prevents the recipient from receiving the message in its original form. Sometimes noise refers to the decibel level within the class, so a noisy class can mean that students fail to hear your instructions, but there are other, subtler, forms of noise and any of these can stop your students from following your instructions. A few examples are listed here:

- **Forgetting equipment.** Although this is annoying, it is a fact of life that students will forget pens, paper, textbooks and other essential equipment. Make sure that you have a reserve supply of these things but do not advertise this fact. Students should not become used to borrowing resources – instead it should be a last resort.
- **Distractions outside the classroom.** This is a very difficult area for any teacher. Distractions outside the classroom inevitably have an impact on what goes on inside the classroom but while it is important that you recognise the impact things outside the classroom have on behaviour, you still need to ensure that students are as focused as possible.
- **Distractions inside the classroom.** At first glance it might seem as though one student is going off task but it is always important to look at the bigger picture and see whether what you are picking up is retaliation or whether a student is being provoked. Often this is very difficult to spot but there are signs to look out for – any smirks, students overly concentrating on their work or disapproving glances from other members of the class.

All of these factors could come under the term 'noise' and so it is important to ensure that you have strategies for each of them. While it is sometimes easy to react to these distractions, never lose your focus as to what is important in the lesson – that is, the learning taking place.

Behaviour management

While eliminating background noise is one part of behaviour management, other forms of action involve strategies to address off-task behaviour by individual students. Later in the chapter we will look at one method of intervention but before that we need to return to the first principles of behaviour management.

Let's go back to the original scenario. Etienne is not completing the work so it is important that we make sure that he gets back to the task. However, the manner in which we do this can influence others within the group. A verbal reminder will be heard by at least some of the group. While this might be a good thing (if you need to 'send a message' to the group), it might indicate to the rest of the group that there has been defiance of your instructions. This can weaken your position and so in some cases teachers try to leave verbal reminders to later on in the intervention tariff.

Before all of this, however, it is important to make sure that the rules for the classroom are clear. Students often have a very clear understanding of the concept of equity and if you enforce rules which they are unaware of, then that tends to lead to increased problems as students see the enforcement as unfair. So, as mentioned in Chapter 13, it is important that the basic ground rules for the class are set down from the start and, most importantly, that they are enforced consistently. You also need to make sure that your instructions are clear. Ending all instructions with a verbal check such as a directed question helps to identify any problems in explanation as well as giving you leverage if a student says that they did not understand the task.

Activity

Another good technique to be aware of is the idea of giving students 'consequences'. This is explained by Cowley (2013) as a way of engaging students with the decision. You explain what will happen if students fail to follow your instructions (so, for example, you would say 'You do realise that if you don't complete the task by the end of the lesson, then you will be given a detention'). This means that there is shared responsibility for the decision. Try coming up with a form of words that will ensure that students know the consequences of their actions in these scenarios:

1. Yuan is constantly talking when you are trying to explain things to the class.
2. Keeley has forgotten her textbook twice in a week.
3. Lotte argues with you constantly when you ask the class to complete a task.

The intervention tariff

The intervention tariff suggests a number of escalating approaches that you can use when managing your classroom. You don't have to start at the beginning – indeed for more serious breaches of classroom discipline you might well go straight to the last intervention – but for most cases, you work your way up from the start to the end.

The first strategy is to give students non-verbal clues. These are ways in which you can let your students know that you have spotted their off-task behaviour without actually drawing it to the attention of the rest of the class. This means that the interaction stays between you and the student and the likelihood is that it does not escalate. There are plenty of strategies that can be used and the activity below will help you practise them:

Activity

Position yourself in front of a mirror - the bigger the better - and practise the following non-verbal clues:

- Maintain eye contact for three seconds, then raise your eyebrows, shake your head and break eye contact (moving your eyes any way other than in a downwards direction)
- If you wear glasses, practise looking over the top of them, again shaking your head and breaking eye contact after three seconds
- Looking into the mirror and making sure that you are not smiling, make a gesture with your hands that might indicate 'stop it' to a student

The second stage of the intervention tariff is proxemic control. This refers to the use of space to control behaviour. Hall (1963) wrote extensively about the fact that people have various spaces around them and as people get closer their senses are generally heightened. Think about how you feel when someone moves closer to you; depending on your relationship with the person moving towards you, it could provoke all sorts of emotions. As a teacher, you can use this to ensure that students know that you have spotted their off-task behaviour.

Figure 14.3 Intervention tariff

Normally we would be in what Hall calls a student's social space. This is an area approximately 1.5 to 3.5 metres from students. Most people are comfortable in these circumstances and will be happy to behave in whatever way they see fit. By moving towards a student who is misbehaving you approach their personal space and this is when students start to feel discomfort and hence start to think about what they are doing.

This is a tactic that needs to be used with a certain degree of caution. Do not move too close to a student as some people will react to any invasion of personal space in an aggressive manner and it is important not to 'invade' personal space. Instead a small movement towards the desk of the student who is misbehaving is often the only thing that is needed. If that does not work then you need to move on to the next stage of the tariff.

Activity

This activity gets you to think about using tone of voice in order to get points across. Often how you say things is just as important as what you say. Some teachers make the mistake of thinking that talking loudly will help them control behaviour but the reality is that this tends to normalise that amount of volume. Instead you need to concentrate on *how* you say things.

Think of three commonly felt emotions and then say the following random words in such a way as to convey that emotion:

apple, table, penny, clock, hippopotamus, banana, paper clip

The last stage is to move on to a final warning. You might decide to use verbal warnings a number of times but at some point, if the behaviour persists, you would move to the final stage.

A final warning should be exactly that, a final attempt to get the student to complete the task. A good idea is to use this stage in conjunction with the consequences approach discussed earlier. If you do issue a final warning, ALWAYS follow through on it. If a student fails to behave in the manner you ask them to then you must follow through with your warning – not to do so would seriously affect your chances of getting students to behave in the future.

The impact of communication

Eric Berne, who is known as the father of Transactional Analysis (often abbreviated to TA), suggested that our behaviour can influence others (Berne, 1964) and that is something else to bear in mind when setting up your classroom management strategy.

TA is study of our interactions and communication with others (referred to as transactions). According to Berne we communicate from a particular 'ego state' which represents a way of being and feeling at a given moment in time and it is suggested that this influences the way we communicate, which in turn has an influence on the response we get from others. The study of transactional analysis is quite literally an analysis of such transactions.

The 'ego state' model has three key parts:

- **Parent** – this conveys the impression of nurturing (or in some cases controlling). There is a strong focus on the observance of rules and also the concept of superiority. This represents things we have learnt from our own parental figures.
- **Adult** – this state is linked to rationality and logic. There is a focus on independence and a calm, thoughtful approach to problem-solving.
- **Child** – when in this state there tends to be a dependency on others and in some situations rebellion against those in charge. This is often considered the most emotional ego state.

A simple way to remember this is as taught (Parent), thought (Adult) and felt (Child).

Reflection

According to the theory, the state we communicate from will influence the person we are communicating with and the likelihood that their communication will be from a corresponding state. For example, if we communicate from a parent state with a comment such as *Remember to put your coat on before you go outside*, we are likely to encourage a response from a child ego state as it is unlikely we would feel the need to give this message to an adult. Think about your reaction to being told to put on your coat. This might range from obedience (you put on your coat) to defiance (I am not being told what to do) but, whatever the reaction, it is likely to align with the child ego state.

Now think about your reaction if someone says, *It was a bit chilly when I went out earlier, what do you think, coat or no coat?* This question is likely to encourage you to think and make a judgement - in effect you are behaving in what we perceive as an adult manner.

Where communication is largely made up of complementary transactions, it is likely to have a familiar and comfortable flow, something which we might want to encourage in a positive classroom. However, communication with others is often more complex than this as a result of misunderstandings or miscommunication which leads to an emotional rather than a rational response. In TA theory, this type of communication is referred to as a 'crossed transaction'. A crossed transaction occurs when the response to your communication does not correspond to the ego state you were communicating from. For example, suppose you ask someone a simple and intentionally innocent question such as *How are you?* and receive a response in the form of a rant: *How am I? How can you ask me that? I have problems that you couldn't even imagine. I can't believe you even asked me that.* In this example the questioner was communicating from an adult ego state, expecting a response from a comparable adult state and received a rather angry child!

Activity

Think about the dialogue below and how it relates to Berne's ego states. Although this might be slightly exaggerated, it does illustrate much of what happens within a classroom. Identify any ego states that appear to be evident during this exchange:

Teacher: Now you did really well in this test, well done. I am very satisfied with your progress.

Student (putting up their hand): Sir! Sir! I have forgotten my textbook.

Teacher: That was a very silly thing to do, now why did you do that?

Student: Dunno

Teacher: OK, we will see what we can do about this later. Now what do you think of the use of dystopian language in the book *1984*?

Student: I think that it can be linked back to current society very closely.

Teacher: That's an interesting viewpoint, what do you mean by that?

The activity shows how we can sometimes shift between states. The complementary communication that was evident at the start of the exchange (did you spot the parent/child transaction?) was replaced by a more adult approach by the end. It would be interesting to see if this mirrors anything that happens within your classroom.

Other factors influencing classroom management

Your behaviour management strategy, your communication skills and the quality of your teaching tend to be the main factors that influence how effective your classroom management is but there are other factors to think about before you start teaching. The following list is designed to get you to think about how you approach your classroom management strategies:

- Think about how students enter the room – have you established a routine so that there is an air of calm each time students enter the room?
- Have you set up the room in a manner conducive to the learning that is planned? If you are doing groupwork are tables bunched? If it is individual work do the position of desks allow for this?
- Are students aware of your rules? In an ideal world, every teacher would follow the same rules but even in the most regimented school, there are differences, so it is important to communicate those rules to students regularly.
- The start of the lesson is crucial. If students are focused at the start, the chances are that they will continue to be focused, so make sure that your starter activity engages students.

Things to think about

Effective classroom management is key to a successful lesson and it is important that you think about it before you start the lesson. Putting in place all of the elements means that you can focus on the lesson and not have to worry about the behaviour of the students. It will also reassure the students – the teachers that are often judged to be the best are the ones who are very clear about their expectations and consistent in their approach. So, have you got your intervention tariff clear in your head? Are you confident with using both proxemic and non-verbal control techniques? Think also about the ego states you adopt – are you aware of the impact of your actions on others? Finally, are you prepared to remove any unnecessary barriers to learning when they appear?

In a nutshell

This feature covers the essentials of effective behaviour management to provide some examples of how these can be used to inform your practice. This resource can be photocopied and used as a revision tool or a prompt for discussion with your peers.

Schramm's communication theory

Schramm (1954) researched how we communicate with each other. He identified a series of roles that people play, notably the encoder (who sends the message) and the decoder (who tries to understand the message). Even in a classroom, our communication tends to be coded – this may be via non-verbal communication or by established confirmations (house points for good work, detentions for poor work). This means that there is always the possibility that messages will be decoded incorrectly.

Another problem is 'noise', which is anything that could stop the decoder correctly hearing the message.

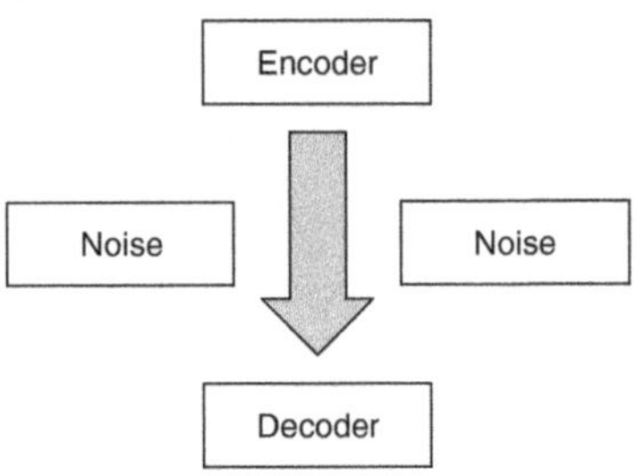

Source: Schramm (1954).

Putting it into practice

STEP ONE
Identify any 'noise' that occurs within your classroom. This could include anything that stops your message reaching its intended recipient.

STEP TWO
Think about the potential problems that noise could cause.

STEP THREE
Identify any solutions that would help reduce noise and ensure that the correct message reaches its destination.

STEP FOUR
Try this out during a class to see if it improves communication within the classroom.

STEP FIVE
Think about alternative strategies to ensure that your message is reinforced so that students receive the same message more than once.

Suggestions for further reading

Cowley, S (2007) *Guerilla Guide to Teaching: The Definitive Resource for New Teachers*. London: Continuum.

Cowley, S (2013) *The Seven C's of Positive Behaviour Management (Alphabet Sevens)*. CreateSpace Independent Publishing Platform.

Rogers, B (2011) *Classroom Behaviour: A Practical Guide to Effective Teaching, Behaviour Management and Colleague Support*. London: Sage.

References

Berne, E (1964) *Games People Play – The Basic Hand Book of Transactional Analysis*. New York: Ballantine Books.

Hall, E (1963) 'A system for the notation of proxemic behaviour', *American Anthropologist*, 65 (5): 1003–26.

Schramm, W (1954) 'How communication works', in W. Schramm (ed.), *The Process and Effects of Communication*. Urbana, IL: University of Illinois Press, pp. 3–26.

15

Checking learners' progress

In this chapter we will explore:

- **the key principles of assessment;**
- **using assessment to enhance learning;**
- **providing constructive feedback.**

Introduction

Checking students' learning is an integral part of teaching. If we don't check understanding of what we are trying to teach, then all we are doing is presenting information which may or may not be received by our learners. Informal assessment, in the form of learning checks, is going on all the time and forms part of the natural interaction between teacher and students. It is a key function of the teaching and learning process and according to Race *et al.* (2005), assessment and the provision of feedback is one of the most important parts of a teacher's role. In this chapter we will consider forms of assessment and how these are used in practice with an emphasis on the ways you can check learners' progress in order to adjust your teaching and provide effective support.

Principles of assessment

Assessment is an accepted part of the learning process and has many purposes. Despite this we tend to focus on the type of assessment which leads to certification rather than the assessments which have the potential to improve our success. In reality, the role of assessment is much wider than this and we assess for a whole range of reasons, including:

- diagnosing specific learning needs;
- identifying gaps in learning;

- evaluating teaching;
- providing corrective feedback and guidance on next steps.

So, assessment is both a measure of what has been taught and what has been learnt. Assessment can be formal and informal and can take place in a variety of ways. There are a number of formal assessment strategies that you will already be familiar with, such as exams, essays and practical tests, as well as a range of informal assessments that you may already employ in your teaching, such as quizzes or questioning. This is a fundamental part of your role and it is worth spending some time familiarising yourself with the variety of assessment activities you may be involved with.

Activity

Look at the following list and decide whether these are formal or informal assessment strategies.

Assignments	Case studies	Examinations
Essays	Presentations	Quizzes
Question and answer	Discussion	Debate
Games	Practical experiments	Concept maps
Reports	Learning logs	Reflective journals
Observation	Portfolios	Posters
Role play	Short answer questions	Research projects

How easy was it to complete that task? It is likely that many of these methods can be used in both formal and informal ways. What influences the formality of the assessment is the impact of it – in short, whether the assessment is a formal assessment **of** learning or whether it is an assessment **for** learning.

Objectivity

One of the recognised difficulties with assessment is the issue of objectivity. In theory, good assessment practice reduces any factors which may lead to a misinterpretation of results. However, it is worth acknowledging that all assessment practice has an element of subjectivity as it normally involves interpretation by humans, who will be influenced by their own views and experiences. While it could be argued that some types of assessment are more objective than others, complete objectivity is likely to be an aspiration rather than a given. For this reason, it is important to consider the ways in which we can increase the validity, reliability and fairness of our assessments.

Validity, reliability and fairness

Validity refers to the accuracy of an assessment in relation to whether it measures what it is supposed to measure. A valid assessment therefore is an assessment which is appropriate for the subject and topic. For example, if you were making an assessment of whether or not someone could ride a bicycle, would you ask them to write an essay about it or would you observe them doing it? Validity in assessment is enhanced if assessors take into account the purpose of the assessment, the material being assessed and the required outcomes of the assessment.

Reliability is the measure of how consistent an assessment is. If an assessment is reliable then it should also be replicable, which means that if taken again by the same group of students it would produce the same results. A number of things can impact on the reliability of a given assessment including the wording of assessment questions or unclear marking guidelines. Addressing those concerns would improve reliability and it is also important that all assessors are interpreting questions and marking guidelines in the same way. One way of doing this is to introduce standardisation as part of the assessment process. This normally involves all assessors marking the same piece of work and then meeting to discuss the assessment decisions. This approach provides the opportunity for assessors to discuss any parts of the assessment where responses might be interpreted differently or where questions/marking guidelines are less clear. Standardisation is common practice for examiners and is used regularly in vocational assessment.

Fairness in assessment simply means that all students will have equal access to the assessment and equal chance of success. In order to be fair, an assessment must also be an accurate reflection of the learning outcomes of a given course. Fairness should take into account an inclusive approach to assessment and recognise that some students, who may be disadvantaged by physical or learning disabilities, should be provided with relevant adjustments to allow them equal access to the assessment opportunity.

Reflective task

Are the assessments in your subject valid, reliable and fair? If not, what could you do to improve them?

Types of assessment

In this chapter we will focus on four types of assessment as these are the most likely to form part of your professional practice.

Summative assessment

Summative assessment has become a key focus for schools and colleges as well as the teachers working in them. It has been argued that this has detracted from the process of teaching and learning by creating a drive towards achievement and encouraging approaches such as teaching to the test, in effect creating what have been termed 'exam factories' (Coffield and Williamson, 2011). This may be

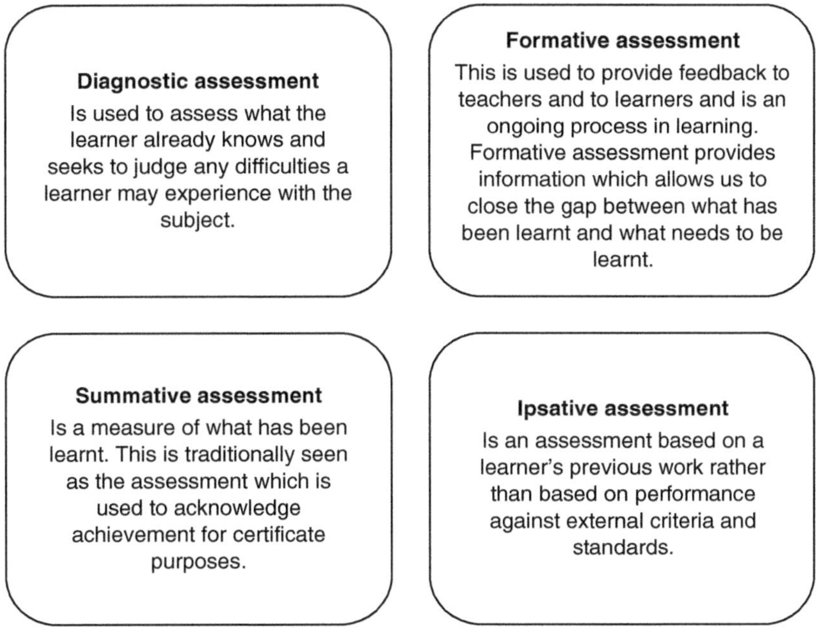

Figure 15.1 Types of assessment chart

an outcome of the introduction of league tables and the increased focus on Ofsted judgements but is also a reflection of society as a whole and as such is something which has a significant influence on our students. Indeed, for many students, learning is judged purely on achieving the best exam results: *From our students' point of view assessment always defines the actual curriculum* (Ramsden, 1992: 187). Remember this when you next hear the question *Are we being assessed on this?* and be aware that while you may very often want to teach things because you think the students will find them interesting or that may be useful in a wider sense, in the students' eyes there is a clear link between learning and assessment and they are likely to be far more motivated if that connection is made clear. That said, this is not a suggestion that teaching to the test is the best approach, simply an assertion that students are more likely to be motivated if they understand *what* they are learning and *why*. For this reason all planning should make reference to relevant assessment.

Formative assessment

The importance that is placed on certified achievement means that we may be in danger of negating the significance of non-summative assessments. Formative assessment encompasses all of the assessment activity which does not lead to final certification; this would include diagnostic assessments and ipsative assessments which suggests that most of our time is spent involved in formative assessments rather than summative. On this basis, it might be reasonable to assume that it is this area, rather than summative assessment, which should consume most of our energies.

Formative assessment provides learners with feedback on their learning and teachers with feedback on their teaching, and according to a study by Black and Wiliam (1998a) effective use of formative assessment should have a positive impact on classroom practice. However, the findings indicated that assessment was used predominantly as a way of comparing students and collecting marks to fill up assessment records rather than using assessment information to discern learning needs. As a result, grading functions are overemphasised at the expense of learning. To remedy this, it is suggested that:

- feedback should focus on the specific qualities of a piece of work, with advice on what can be done to improve;
- learners should be encouraged to self-assess so that they gain an understanding of the purpose of their learning and what they need to do to improve;
- learners should be given opportunities to discuss their understanding within every lesson;
- tests and homework activities should be clear and relevant to learning aims.

Figure 15.2 Formative assessment

Using assessment to enhance learning

Assessment should be an ongoing process within a teaching and learning context and as such needs to form a part of every lesson. If we are not using formative assessment as part of teaching, we are not really teaching at all, we are simply presenting or delivering information for consumption.

Figure 15.3 Assessment for learning

Diagnostic assessment

An important aspect of any assessment is that it provides information which can lead to improved performance. Initially we can use diagnostic assessments to establish current levels of knowledge which will inform longer-term planning as well as the ways in which we might differentiate to support individual students. We can then build on this picture by using regular checks on learning to establish what gaps there are in students' knowledge. There are a number of diagnostic tests which cover various aspects of learning; sometimes these relate to generic skills such as literacy and numeracy, particularly if they underpin success in a particular topic. Other diagnostic tests aim to gauge base knowledge in a particular subject. You should be guided by your colleagues in relation to the types of diagnostic tests available but it might also be worth reading around the topic for your own benefit as this is a crucial step in establishing your learners' needs.

Learning checks

As well as providing you with information, learning checks are a way of ensuring that learners are actively involved in the lesson and can be both fun and challenging. The list of potential activities is limited only by your access to resources and your imagination, and there are numerous online resources available which can be adapted for this purpose. To get you started here are ten activities you can use to check learning.

1. **Question and answer.** Don't underestimate this technique – it is quick, easy and can be adapted to individual learners. This can be used several times in any lesson.
2. **Quizzes.** These may be paper-based or use a web-based template and are usually used to sum up a chunk of learning.
3. **Pose a question.** This is an opportunity to introduce peer assessment. Give out 'pose a question' cards to each student, then allow them some time to think about what they have learnt in the class and write down a question based on this. Each student then needs to pick someone else in the class to ask the question of.
4. **Game show.** If you want to introduce a fun competitive element, there are a number of free templates for games such as *Who Wants to Be a Millionaire?* or *Blockbusters*, which are named after the popular television programmes and can be populated with questions around any topic.
5. **Empty outlines** (sometimes referred to as gapped handouts). This is a simple resource that is easy to adapt to any topic. You provide an outline of the key learning points and the learners have to fill in the gaps, you can go through the answers in the class, or if you want to provide more specific feedback, take in the answers and go through them in the next class.
6. **Hot seat.** This is a variation on question and answer but allows you to prepare thought-provoking questions before the class. Place questions on random seats throughout the room. When prompted, students check their seats and answer the questions. If there are some students who don't have a question they can be involved in peer assessment of the answers.
7. **Human line-up.** This is a useful strategy for any assessment activity that links to a continuum. For example, you may want to ask questions related to periods in history and could label one side of the room as 'pre-historic', the centre as 'middle ages' and the other side as '20th century'. Students then go to the relevant spot on the continuum to answer their question. This is also useful as a reflective activity whereby students can be asked where they might place themselves from 'novice' to 'expert' against a given topic.
8. **Four corners.** This activity is useful to help learners to clarify their thinking. Use a question which may have a range of responses and have four potential choices in response to the question, placed in each corner of the room. After posing the question, ask the learners to respond by moving to one of the four corners. Once the choice is made, the groups in each corner should discuss their reasons for making the choice.
9. **Concept maps.** This is a useful activity to carry out in small groups or as a whole class. Draw the key topic in the middle of the map on a piece of flipchart paper or on the board. Then ask for volunteers to write a key point on the map. Each time a volunteer adds to the map they show, and explain, how their point links to others.
10. **Sticky note pointers.** This is a simple activity to provide you with information on what students still have to learn. Use different coloured sticky notes and give two to each of the students at the end of the lesson. Ask them to write one thing they have learnt on one colour and one thing they are not clear on or would like to know more about on another. The students simply leave these in an allocated place and you can review them before the next lesson.

Activity

Think about the ten learning checks we have presented and write down your ideas for how you could adapt one or more of these for your teaching. If you are keeping a reflective journal this might be a useful entry for it as it will allow you the scope to think about the theory underpinning the practice of using learning checks.

Ipsative assessment

This type of assessment is a way of comparing yourself against previous performance and is often used in conjunction with setting individual targets. The use of ipsative assessment allows you to really personalise the assessment process and supports your learners in achieving their specific aims. The level of personalisation is more likely to help learners act on the feedback they are given and helps to improve confidence as it allows opportunities to log and reward progress, something which is often lost in whole-class approaches.

Activity

Make a list of all the ways in which you do (or could) make use of opportunities for ipsative assessment. When you have your list, think about the ways in which you can build this into your everyday teaching.

Creative approaches to assessment

There are many forms of assessment that will be familiar to all of us, for example exams, essays, multiple choice questions and presentations. These are well known because they are customary in our education system. Many are prescribed by qualification-awarding bodies and others are simply the result of everyday practice. One concern with 'traditional' assessments is that they tend to suit more traditional learners and do not necessarily bring out the best in everyone. While some of the assessments you use may be set (this is particularly the case with many summative assessments), there are others where you have a degree of control and this is an opportunity to take a more creative approach.

Many assessments are based on a written approach which has the advantage of being easy to assess as well as providing an insight into important generic skills such as literacy. However this immediately creates barriers for learners with dyslexia, which affects around 10 per cent of the population (British Dyslexia Association, 2017, online). Written assessments are also limited in their ability to provide feedback on wider skills such as discussion or visual presentation of information, so it is important to consider using a range of strategies to ensure that your assessment approach is varied and provides opportunities for everyone to shine. Every tutor will have different opportunities and limitations in relation to assessment so it is not possible to provide a definitive list of assessments. However, the following may be a starting point as it outlines nine ways to assess which don't have a focus on the written word.

1. **Artefacts.** The dictionary definition of 'artefact' refers to something made or given shape by man. Learners could be asked to create an artefact to demonstrate their understanding of a particular topic and then share their ideas with others in the class. One way to do this is to present a key learning point then provide learners with a set of resources (modelling clay, crayons, paper,

glue, pipe cleaners . . . anything to hand) and ask them to create something which represents their understanding of what they have learnt. This is a really useful way of getting your learners to construct their own meaning as they will be forced into judging new learning against what they already know and will have to analyse this information in relation to what is similar or different.

2. **Blogs.** Learners could use a blog to explain and share their understanding of a particular topic. Using this method may encourage research into the topic and will mean that the information has to be analysed in order to rework it into a blog format. Creating a blog does require some technical knowledge so it is worth making sure you try this out before using it as a strategy.
3. **Comic strips.** Getting learners to produce a comic strip allows them to analyse the key points of new learning in order to represent it in pictorial form. Producing a comic strip also requires them to sequence the learning which may help them to remember it more effectively. It is important to emphasise that this is not a test of drawing, so you may want to consider providing some things which can be cut out and added to the strip, or you could suggest the use of simple stick drawings.
4. **Collage.** Creating a collage is a way of presenting information visually and requires learners to select key information to represent their understanding of a topic. It may be worth including rules to ensure that links between parts of information are clear.

Figure 15.4 Chicken blog

5. **Podcasts.** Creating a podcast is a really useful way of getting across a message through voice (although video can also be included). Getting learners to do this will not only increase their IT skills, it will also ensure they have to think through and plan what they are going to say and as a result will need to make sense of new information. Like blogging, this does require a small amount of technical knowledge so it is important to prepare beforehand.

6. **Poster presentations.** This allows learners to present information in a visual format in a similar way to a collage. As there is no particular format for a poster it is important to provide guidelines about size and content. Learners should then be asked to present their posters (in the same way that they might do a Microsoft PowerPoint presentation) to the rest of the group.

7. **Scrapbooks.** This is a really useful activity for ongoing assessment and is a very simple approach. You could ask learners to start a scrapbook at the beginning of an academic year or the beginning of a unit and to collect information which demonstrates their developing understanding. This could be articles, headlines, images, etc. The beauty of the scrapbook is that it evolves alongside the learning, and because it is not intended to be pristine, can be annotated and changed as learning develops. For those who would prefer to keep their scrapbooks electronically this can be done using something like Dropbox.

8. **Video essays.** This provides learners with the opportunity to represent their information in visual and audio form. Simple videos can be created using phones, tablets or small hand-held recorders and can easily be shared via a dedicated course YouTube account.

9. **Simulations.** This provides learners with an opportunity to practise in a simulated environment and can be done practically or electronically (there are a number of free simulated games online). A practical simulation might involve setting up a realistic activity whereby learners have to complete a series of steps in a process or role play a specific interaction.

Really there is no limit to the range of strategies you can use. It just requires a little thought and planning.

Providing constructive feedback

According to Hattie's (2009) study on the impact of instructional techniques, formative assessment, specifically corrective feedback, has a significant impact on students' learning so building in opportunities to provide feedback should have a positive impact on your teaching. For this to be effective, feedback should be connected to learning goals as *the main purpose of feedback is to reduce the gap between current understandings and performance and a goal* (Hattie and Timperley, 2007: 86). In this model, feedback must therefore be linked to three questions.

1. **Where am I going?** What are the goals?

2. **How am I going?** What progress is being made towards the goal?

3. **Where to next?** What activities need to be undertaken to make better progress?

(Hattie and Timperley, 2007)

This model is very similar to the idea of feedback and feedforward which was outlined in Chapter 5 and there are several ways you can structure your approach to this.

Approaches to structuring feedback

Using a 'medals and missions' approach ensures that you outline what learners have done well and provide constructive criticism in the form of a goal. The medal is an acknowledgement of what the learner has done well and can focus on the process as well as the outcome, for example: *You worked hard on this task and produced a detailed poster.* The mission links to a specific goal for the individual learner: *You could think about how you worked within the group rather than focusing on your part of the task.* This is a very simple way of providing balanced feedback. A similar strategy you could try is the 'feedback sandwich' which works on the basis of praising what has been done well, followed by information about what could have been better. This section provides the key content in relation to closing knowledge gaps as it focuses on any misunderstandings or inaccuracies. Finally, the sandwich is closed on a further note of praise which is intended to provide motivation for the learner.

Figure 15.5 Feedback sandwich

A note of caution

Feedback is an essential part of the learning process and has a very specific role in addressing misconceptions as well as acknowledging achievements. Using a 'formulaic' approach to structuring feedback certainly has its uses but it is not something which must be followed slavishly. If for example, you have a learner who struggled with an assessment and didn't seem to try very hard to overcome that struggle, would the use of a praise sandwich be appropriate? Or would it be better to provide honest and constructive feedback which highlights that improvements are necessary and, with some effort, are possible? A key component of feedback is that it is honest and specific and, for these reasons, models used to structure feedback must be adapted to the work being assessed.

Things to think about

In what ways could you use assessment to close the gap between what your learners already know and what they need to learn? Is it important to use a range of assessment strategies in order to meet the needs of individual learners and, if so, how can you adapt what you do to ensure this happens? When you started reading this chapter you may have had very clear views on the purpose of assessment and the ways in which you should use it in your teaching practice. It is possible that the scope of assessment approaches was not something you had thought much about but now you should have a range of ideas which can help you to help your learners through the use of effective assessment and feedback.

In a nutshell

This feature covers the key principles of checking learning and provides some strategies you can use in your practice. This resource can be photocopied and used as a revision tool or a prompt for discussion with your peers.

Using assessment to enhance learning

Black and Wiliam (1998b) suggest that formative assessment has more effect on learning than any other factor and that many teachers do not adopt good practice as they often mimic summative assessment strategies within formative assessment. The following suggestions outline ideas for effective formative assessment.

Avoid grading
Grades tend to demotivate low attainers and don't challenge high attainers. So avoid grading (unless this is a requirement).

Use self-assessment
Self-assessment encourages reflection, ensures students take responsibility for their learning and can focus attention on the criteria for success.

Give learning-centred feedback
Use 'medals' and 'missions' to outline what has been done well and what needs to improve. This makes the focus on how to improve performance.

Use assessment to 'find faults and fix'
Use teaching methods which provide opportunities to check what students can and can't do, then plan strategies to address any difficulties.

Putting it into practice

Some ideas to try...

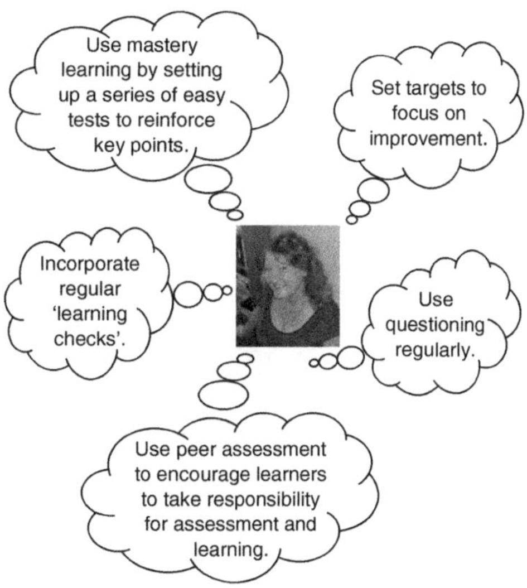

Source: Black and Wiliam (1998b).

Suggestions for further reading

Race, P, Brown, S and Smith, B (2005) *500 Tips on Assessment*, 2nd edn. London: Routledge.

References

Black, P and Wiliam, D (1998a) *Inside the Black Box: Raising Standards Through Classroom Assessment*. London: GL Assessment.

Black, P and Wiliam, D (1998b) 'Assessment and classroom learning', *Assessment in Education*, 5 (1): 7–71.

British Dyslexia Association: http://www.bdadyslexia.org.uk (accessed 30 June 2017).

Coffield, F and Williamson, B (2011) *From Exam Factories to Communities of Discovery: The Democratic Route*. London: IoE Press.

Hattie, J (2009) *Visible Learning: A Synthesis of Over 800 Meta-analyses Related to Achievement*. London: Routledge.

Hattie, J and Timperley, H (2007) 'The power of feedback', *Review of Educational Research*, 77 (1): 81–112.

Race, P, Brown, S and Smith, B (2005) *500 Tips on Assessment*, 2nd edn. London: Routledge.

Ramsden, P (1992) *Learning to Teach in Higher Education*. London: Routledge.

16

Pastoral care

In this chapter we will explore:

- **the pastoral role;**
- **setting goals for development;**
- **recognising boundaries.**

Introduction

It is easy to think of pastoral care as an 'add on' to the teacher's role as it often takes place outside the classroom and has a focus on things which do not always have a direct impact on learning. If this is your initial view, think again! Although the pastoral role initially has a focus on social and emotional well-being, it also has a very definite connection with a learner's readiness for learning as well as their ability to apply themselves to learning activities. Subsequently the pastoral role also has an impact on inclusivity as it allows a more personalised approach for each learner. In this chapter we will explore what the pastoral role entails as well as what it doesn't, and will consider approaches to organising and managing one-to-one meetings as well as setting individual goals with learners.

What does the pastoral role involve?

Although organisations may differ in their approach, the pastoral role undertaken by teachers usually refers to both academic and personal support (although in some cases the roles are separated). In a sense, it is the bridge between barriers to learning and achievement. In Chapter 13 we discussed the ways in which teachers help to create a positive classroom and considered the different dimensions of learning outlined by Illeris (2009). These were referred to as the content dimension, the incentive dimension and the interaction dimension which together made up the learning environment. In other words, we need to consider not only what we are teaching but also how and in what context, as learning also has a social and emotional impact on learners. This is not always recognised in larger teaching groups, making the role of the personal/academic support tutor essential in keeping learners on track.

A personal or academic tutorial is based around a one-to-one meeting between teacher and student and is usually linked to providing a personalised approach to teaching, learning and support. Most often, the role is supported by specific documentation and is closely linked to the setting of goals and targets. Its purpose is to alleviate barriers to learning and to provide support and challenge to learners. The process is built around four key areas: building relationships, creating a framework of support, providing academic guidance and signposting to other sources of support.

Figure 16.1 Striding to success

Approaches to organising one-to-one meetings

One-to-one tutorials are normally scheduled into the weekly timetable, so your first task will be simply to allocate time slots to individual learners. You then need to take into account any paperwork which needs to be completed as part of the process. It is important that this part of the meeting is not the whole focus so you need to make yourself familiar with the paperwork beforehand to allow you to focus your attention fully on the student.

Activity

Find out what the tutorial process is in your setting or placement. You can do this by talking to your mentor or supervisor and looking at the intranet for any policies or guidance notes. Familiarise yourself with all of the paperwork and check anything you are not sure of. Some things to consider might be:

- How long should a tutorial be?
- How much detail is required on the documentation?
- If targets are being set, is there a specific number required?
- Whose responsibility is it to keep the paperwork?
- How does the process fit in with planning for lessons?

Other considerations are to think about where the tutorial will take place – is there an allocated room or are you using a classroom? If the latter, how will you ensure that other students (or staff) do not disrupt the meeting? You may also need to take into account the organisation's guidelines in relation to safeguarding. Often, the recommendation is to hold one-to-one meetings in an open area but this also needs to be balanced with the need to ensure that the student feels safe to discuss whatever concerns they might have.

Egan's skilled helper model

This is a three-stage model developed to help people solve problems and develop opportunities. It is based on three key questions:

- What is going on?
- What do I want instead?
- How might I get what I want?

As its focus is on empowering the individual, it fits very well within the personal and academic tutorial process and the three questions are easy to adapt to many of the concerns which students may encounter, for example:

- What is going on? *I am worried about meeting assignment deadlines.*
- What do I want instead? *To have my work finished with time to check it before submission.*
- How might I get what I want? *I need to think about how I am organising my time and how much I should allocate to completing assignments.*

It is unlikely that all interactions will be quite as simple as the illustration provided. For example, will all students immediately be able to establish the link between scheduling and meeting deadlines? Is every student likely to acknowledge that managing time is their responsibility? In order to establish useful actions it might be worth exploring initial responses to establish why the problem has arisen in the first place and what strategies can be put in place to ensure that it isn't a problem that continually reoccurs. Considering Egan's model in three stages might be helpful here:

- **Stage 1** – Explores 'the story' – what is going on?
- **Stage 2** – Considers any 'blind spots' – what is really going on?
- **Stage 3** – Investigates ways of focusing and prioritising approaches and will be linked to ways in which changes can be put in place through the use of specific goals.

Figure 16.2 Blind spot

The model was originally developed for counselling and therapy settings and its main aim is to help people to manage problems more effectively. While we are not recommending that you take on the role of the counsellor, we are aware that counselling skills are a very important part of the teacher's role and having a framework to support this is very useful. In Egan's words, the model can be defined as a way of *helping people become better at helping themselves* . . . (Egan, 1998: 7–8).

The skilled helper model is based on the principle of applying the skills of questioning and active listening and works best if used in an environment in which the student feels secure and valued. This necessarily means building some rapport with individual students which can be difficult when your relationship with them has been shaped by the hierarchical structures present within education settings and when you also take on the role of class teacher. This doesn't mean that you have to be 'best friends' with every student and it is important to maintain appropriate boundaries, but it does mean that you need to give some thought to the things which will aid or inhibit communication. There is no foolproof way of creating rapport with another person and we would be reticent to propose a 'one size fits all' approach but there are some behaviours which might be useful in the early stages:

- Leaning slightly towards and making eye contact with the other person to show that you are focused on what they have to say. In doing so, it is also important to remember personal and cultural boundaries.
- Smiling and using 'reinforcers' such as nodding and gestures to provide positive feedback when the other person is talking.
- Building on the other person's ideas to show that you are listening to them. This can be done by paraphrasing, reflecting back and adding questions or ideas.

Figure 16.3 Active listening

Reflection

What conflicts might exist between your role as class teacher and personal/academic support tutor? In what ways can you minimise these conflicts?

Setting goals for development

Research suggests that setting specific goals helps us to achieve our aims (Bandura and Schunk, 1981; Locke and Latham, 1990) and that there are several principles to effective goal-setting. These are:

- clarity
- challenge
- commitment
- feedback
- task complexity.

(Locke and Latham, 1990)

The first of these ensures that our goals are specific and clearly measurable and the second that they are challenging enough to be interesting. A typical concern with goal-setting in education settings is that the process is not valued because it is seen as a 'box-ticking' activity, whereby both parties are compliant in setting goals with minimum challenge. So, if you want your students to value the process ensure that the goals you devise together include challenge and purpose. Part of the process of writing down specific goals is that we are committing to them and it is very helpful if the documentation used to record goals also includes a way of reviewing progress so that you can provide feedback. The use of SMART goals (outlined in Chapter 5) will be very helpful here. Using this approach, you will also ensure that any complexity in the specific tasks will be broken down in order to produce goals with are specific, measurable, realistic and time-constrained.

The GROW model

The GROW model (Whitmore, 2003) is an alternative structure for setting development goals and takes into account the Goal, the current Reality, any Options (or Obstacles) and the Way forward. There are similarities to Egan's skilled helper model in that it is based on the assumption that the current situation requires some changes. The key difference is that this model is based on a coaching approach which it could be argued has a much more specific focus on development and less of a focus on exploring the reasons behind barriers to change.

If you are using this approach to structure personal or academic tutorials it may be worth developing a question bank you can use to get started. Some examples are:

Goal

- What things do you want to work on?
- What do you want to achieve in this subject?
- What would be the perfect outcome for you?

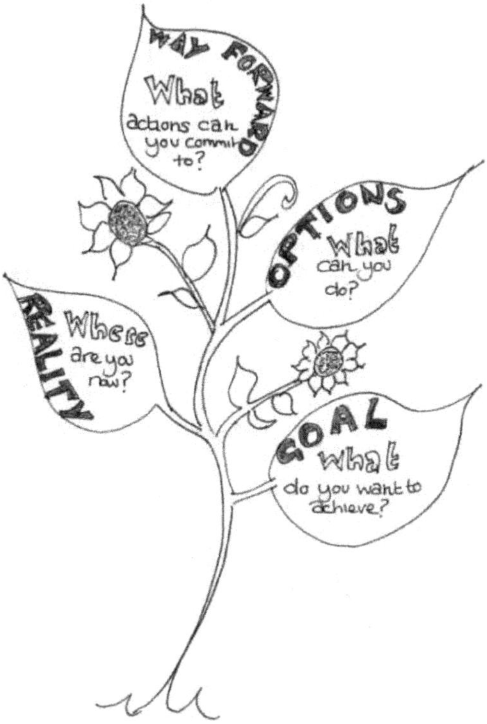

Figure 16.4 GROW model

Reality

- How would you rate your current progress/situation?
- What skills and knowledge have you gathered so far?
- What is working well/less well at the moment?

Options

- What could you do differently?
- What else could you do?
- Give me three potential options . . .

Way forward

- Which of these options will work best for you?
- Who can provide support in achieving these goals?
- What actions will you take now?

Recognising boundaries

Although it is important to create a comfortable environment in which students feel safe enough to share potentially difficult information, it is also key to acknowledge the boundaries that exist within pastoral relationships. It is easy to think that creating boundaries will limit the extent to which you can build rapport and generate trust but in fact it is likely to do the opposite. Boundaries are simply guidelines which allow both parties to be comfortable with the extent of the relationship. They reinforce the purpose of the relationship and recognise its limitations as well as acknowledging that additional expertise may be required should the need arise. The best way to establish boundaries is to start as you mean to go on – you can do this by explaining the purpose of the tutorial and the role each of you will play in it and (if meetings are not centrally timetabled) clarifying how you can be contacted and the limits of your availability.

One boundary in the personal and academic tutorial meeting is to acknowledge when additional or alternative support might be required. The best way to do this is to maintain awareness about any of the issues that may come up in a one-to-one meeting. If any of these seem to extend beyond the norm, then you may wish to speak to the additional student support departments within your organisation. Remember it is not your responsibility to solve all the problems of your students, but it is your responsibility to ensure they get the right support and sometimes that means accepting that you are not the person to provide it.

Figure 16.5 Boundaries

Safeguarding

Safeguarding and promoting the welfare of children and vulnerable adults is everyone's responsibility and is something that is (and should be) taken very seriously in schools and colleges. It refers to a responsibility to protect others from harm as well as taking action to enable the best outcomes for them. This is a priority for all organisations and as such you should be provided with specific training and guidance about what to do if you are concerned about an individual.

Some aspects of safeguarding which may be addressed through the personal and academic tutorial process are those which relate to encouraging students to take responsibility for their own safety and well-being as well as ensuring that attention is paid to any school- or college-wide guidelines in relation to safeguarding. This also offers an opportunity to address any concerns in relation to behaviours which may make others feel unsafe, such as not showing respect for the beliefs and values of those who are different from ourselves.

Key principles related to the safeguarding of others are prevention, protection and support. At a strategic level all education organisations should have in place policies and procedures which provide protection to all members of the organisation and should establish a culture in which safeguarding issues are minimised. For example, classrooms should be positive and safe environments, teaching should be inclusive and vigilant of potential concerns and support should be accessible. Such procedures help prevent safeguarding issues and should provide protection to everyone in the organisation. It is also important that support is available to both students and staff and information about this should be openly shared.

Safeguarding is often a concern for new teachers and it is helpful to familiarise yourself with the relevant guidelines. It is also useful to work on the premise that you are not expected to know everything, so if you are unsure about anything in relation to safeguarding, make sure you speak to someone who can advise you – most schools and colleges will have a named person who can advise on safeguarding issues.

Activity

Try to find your organisation's policy and procedures in relation to safeguarding. Read through these and think about any potential situations which may concern you; for example, what if I suspect one of my learners is being bullied? Arrange a meeting with your mentor to talk through your 'what if?' list.

Things to think about

The tutorial process is a key element of the teaching role and ensures that personalised support can be provided to all learners. In what ways could you prepare yourself to carry out the tutorial role in a structured and supportive way? Is it useful to have a framework to work within? Is there anything you can prepare before your first tutorial to ensure it goes smoothly? When you started reading this chapter you probably had an awareness of the tutorial process, if only from your own experiences of being a student. You should now have some tools which will help you to structure tutorials in ways which will be supportive to your own students and will help them to work towards their individual goals.

In a nutshell

This feature covers the key principles of the GROW model and provides some strategies you can use in your practice. This resource can be photocopied and used as a revision tool or a prompt for discussion with your peers.

The GROW Model

This is a simple model for assisting others to set realistic development goals. It is based on the following elements:

GOAL	What things do you want to work on? What do you want to achieve in this subject? What would be the perfect outcome for you?
REALITY	How would you rate your current progress/situation? What skills and knowledge have you gathered so far? What is working well/less well at the moment?
OPTIONS	What could you do differently? What else could you do? Give me three potential options . . .
WAY FORWARD	Which of these options will work best for you? Who can provide support in achieving these goals? What actions will you take now?

Source: Whitmore (2003).

Putting it into practice

- Ask, don't tell. Use questions to elicit information.
- Practise active listening. Let the learner do the talking.
- Use paraphrasing to test your understanding of the story.
- Explore all the options for a way forward.
- Get commitment to agreed goals. Write them down!
- Explore blind spots through the use of questions and examples.
- Use metaphors to illustrate ideas or provide examples.

Personal development goals

Use this space to set some initial goals for yourself. Don't be too ambitious – there will be plenty of time for that as your training progresses. Try to be specific, so think about what the goal will 'look like' when you have achieved it and how it will be measured.

Goals and deadlines *(What do you want to achieve? By when?)*	

Strategies *(How will you achieve these goals?)*

Success *(How will you know you have achieved the goal(s)?)*

Suggestions for further reading

Egan, G (1998) *The Skilled Helper – A Problem Management Approach to Helping*. Pacific Grove, CA: Brooks-Cole.

References

Bandura, A and Schunk, DH (1981) 'Cultivating competence, self-efficacy, and intrinsic interest through proximal self-motivation', *Journal of Personality and Social Psychology*, 41: 586–98.

Department for Education (2016) *Keeping Children Safe in Education: Statutory Guidance for Schools and Colleges*. London: DFE Publications

Egan, G (1998) *The Skilled Helper – A Problem Management Approach to Helping*. Pacific Grove, CA: Brooks-Cole.

Illeris, K (ed.) (2009) *Contemporary Theories of Learning: Learning Theorists . . . in Their Own Words*. Oxford: Routledge

Locke, EA and Latham, GP (1990) *A Theory of Goal Setting and Task Performance*. Englewood Cliffs, NJ: Prentice Hall.

Whitmore, J (2003) *Coaching for Performance*. London: Nicholas Brealey.

Part 3

Continuing your learning

In this section you will be thinking about your continued professional development as well as ways in which you can work in collaboration with other professionals.

The following chapters will explore:

- **the importance of collaboration;**
- **ways of sharing knowledge with others;**
- **getting your first job;**
- **positive approaches to your teaching role.**

17

Sharing your knowledge with others

In this chapter we will explore:

- **the importance of working with others both inside and outside the organisation;**
- **how to build communities of practice;**
- **how peer observations can benefit your professional practice.**

Introduction

Within your own classroom, it is very easy to believe that you are on your own when it comes to teaching and, in fact, that has been the traditional approach in British education. In some schools, teachers have a base room that they are free to decorate themselves and from which they teach the majority of their lessons. While this has many advantages in terms of encouraging teachers to take pride in their learning environments and in ensuring that resources are kept together, the concern is that it encourages teachers to retreat into their individual classrooms (which are sometimes described using the metaphor of a 'silo') and fail to collaborate. The advantages of moving out of your own classroom and sharing ideas with others are clear. Firstly, it allows you to look at new and different ways of teaching so that your teaching doesn't become stale and, secondly, it allows others to share your good practice.

The importance of working with others

The philosopher Alfred Korzybski talked about how 'the map is not the territory' (Korzybski, 1958). At first, he was talking about the way in which an object and the visual representation of an object (such as a map representing how the land lies) were not necessarily the same thing. But in time the saying began to be used to illustrate how there is not just a single perspective on things and if we believe that there is only one approach then our learning will stagnate and we will fail to embrace new opportunities. If teachers fail to get out of their own classrooms and share good practice with others, there is a danger that they will only see one point of view and neglect alternative approaches.

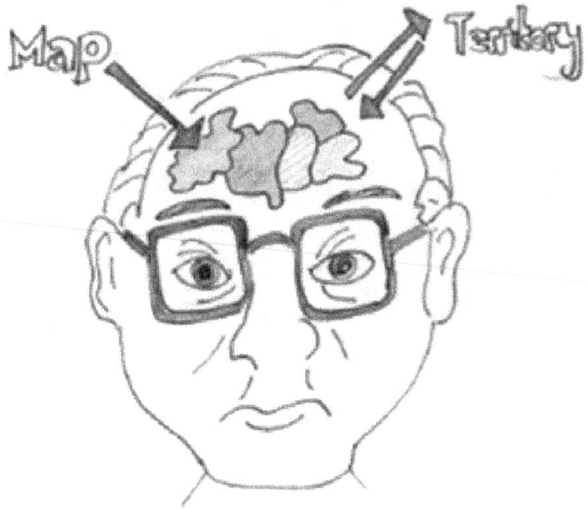

Figure 17.1 The map is not the territory

This chapter is designed to offer a number of suggestions to encourage you to abandon the safety of your own classroom and find ways of sharing good practice with and from others.

Reflection

Below is Standard 8 of the Qualified Teaching Standards.

Think about how you would meet each part of it. The overall title refers to 'fulfilling wider professional responsibilities' while the subheadings are as follows:

- make a positive contribution to the wider life and ethos of the school;
- develop effective professional relationships with colleagues, knowing how and when to draw on advice and specialist support;
- deploy support staff effectively;
- take responsibility for improving teaching through appropriate professional development, responding to advice and feedback from colleagues;
- communicate effectively with parents with regard to pupils' achievements and well-being.

(DfE, 2011)

What is noticeable is that all of these headings refer to interaction with others and, although this can be a difficult activity, it is vital in order to continue to improve as a teacher.

Communities of practice and the importance of making time

The biggest obstacle to sharing knowledge with others is often a perceived lack of time. The life of a teacher is a busy one and things that are not seen as having a direct impact on the students are often neglected, yet the benefits of sharing good practice have been noted by many researchers. Lave and Wenger (1991) described how, in many other walks of life, we learn and work together in a collaborative manner and this could equally be applied to our working life. A decade later, Wenger and Snyder (2000) argued that meeting fellow professionals and creating what they termed a 'community of practice' enabled expertise to be transferred across organisations, encouraging the discussion of effective solutions to a range of problems. These communities do not have to be formal in nature – indeed in many ways an informal sharing of good practice has more benefits as it is seen as something that people choose to do rather than are told to do. In addition, it can occur anyway and at any time rather than being seen as something that has to occur at a set time and place.

A community of practice can also create a sense of a team among members of the organisation that is not always present. Wenger *et al.* (2002) stressed the importance of this part of the community and talked about how it fostered an understanding of each other's roles. This means that when one person needs help, an atmosphere is created whereby the person who needs help is supported.

Activity

List all of the occasions when you are at work but not directly teaching or prepping your lessons. This is likely to be a fairly short list and it might well include: time taken for drinking coffee or eating a sandwich, staff meetings, Open Day preparation as well as a number of other activities.

Once the list is complete, think about ways in which you can share good practice during these activities. Some potential ideas are in team meetings or inviting colleagues for a coffee to talk about ideas.

Online communities

The growth of social media has provided a massive opportunity for sharing ideas and it has the potential to have national, even international, impact! The host of many of these communities of practice is Twitter so it is worth finding your way around this so that you can make the best use of it. It is very easy to set up a Twitter account which will include your username and a profile. You then choose who to follow – this can be individuals, interest groups or organisations. 'Tweets' take the form of 140-character messages which force people to be brief, but you can include web links and photographs. Some groups are subject-specific – so, for example, the hashtag **#teamenglish** gives access to a Dropbox full of resources and the shared wisdom of 7,000 other English teachers that can be used in the teaching of the subject, while others such as **#ukedchat** are generic and aimed at supporting all teachers across a variety of subjects.

Of course, it is important to be critically aware when accessing resources or advice online. Just because a resource or strategy was recommended doesn't always make it right for you (or in some cases it might not even provide the correct answer!) so although the sharing of resources and the support of others online can be valuable, just be careful out there! Also remember that this is a public forum and forms part of your professional profile – what you tweet will be seen by others so make sure you are happy with it.

As well as Twitter, there are a number of other useful sites that provide extra information and support for you. The *TES* website (**tes.com**) provides a lot of good-quality materials while each exam board tends to provide some exemplar material for the syllabus you are teaching.

Researching while teaching

One area that is often neglected by teachers is the area of research-informed practice. In the busy life of a teacher it is often difficult to find the time to undertake research but it can offer a valuable way of broadening your horizons as well as sharing good practice. Research-informed teaching means that we try to ground what we teach in published research rather than merely following the selected textbook. Researching your area is a great way of staying up to date with the latest debates but also helps you understand the topics in a deeper manner. It can lead to you being asked to present your research at conferences which is another good way of networking with fellow professionals.

Figure 17.2 Action research

One form of research that many teachers use, either formally or informally, is action research. This is an approach that links reflective practice to professional practice with the aim of improving teaching within the classroom. The term was first used by Lewin (1946) and although there are a number of differing definitions, the most common one refers to it being a cyclical process that asks you to reflect on your own teaching and identify an area of improvement. The next step of the research is to change something about your professional practice and see if it is improved by the change. This is then evaluated and a new cycle can begin with a view to continuously improving your teaching. In reality, this is a process you are likely to go through anyway when you are teaching but what Lewin and others have done is to formalise the process.

The benefits of peer observation

While on your teacher training course, there is a strong likelihood that you will be asked to observe other teachers. This can be immensely beneficial to your own teaching as it represents a great opportunity to look at other professionals and see what you can learn from them. Teaching is an unusual profession in that much of what we do takes place behind closed doors and this means that the opportunities to learn alternative ways of doing things are limited.

Figure 17.3 Peer observation

Where possible it is a good idea to try to continue this practice when you qualify, but rather than merely wandering into other classrooms randomly, consider how you are going to carry out the observation and what you are looking to get out of it. There are a number of things to think about.

The golden rules of peer observation

1. **Talk to the person you are observing, don't just go into their classroom.** Teachers are often very protective of their classrooms and it requires a degree of trust to be allowed in. Make sure that they are happy for you to be there and explain what you want to get out of the observation.
2. **Identify a focus for the observation and link it to your own professional development.** Think about your own strengths and weaknesses and then think about how a peer observation can help that. It could be that you are struggling to teach a particular subject in a creative way so maybe think about a colleague who you know is creative and see how they are teaching it.
3. **Avoid a 'tick-box' approach.** It is very easy to find a list of 'things to look for' in an observation but the problem with this is that it becomes a rather instrumental experience with you spotting things rather than reflecting on what you see.
4. **The best reflection often comes after the event.** It is very easy to do the peer observation and then rush off to your next appointment without thinking about what you have seen. Schedule in some time for reflection, think through what you have seen and try to understand 'why' things happened rather than focusing on 'what' happened.
5. **Giving feedback** – it is polite to ask the teacher you are observing whether they would like to receive feedback but always remember the purpose of the observation. Peer observations should never be judgemental in nature; rather they are developmental and what you need to do is ensure that you discuss the lesson with your colleague to help you both understand what went on and help inform future practice.

Activity

The second of the golden rules is key to your own development, so this activity is designed to get you thinking about how to make the most of your next peer observation.

On a new piece of paper reflect on your strengths and weaknesses as a teacher. You could link this to feedback you have received or just your own thoughts and feelings.

Once you have completed the activity, identify one strength and one thing that you would wish to improve in your teaching. When you are happy with this, think about how you might promote the strength and who in your organisation would help you most to improve the weakness. It might be somebody who is particularly good at the activity highlighted; alternatively it might be somebody whose opinions you value.

Set up a double peer observation with your chosen person. Ask if you could sit in on one of their lessons and offer them the chance to come into your class to see you at work. Remember that the purpose of this is to learn from the observation, so leave time to reflect on how your own teaching could be adapted as a result of what you have learnt.

Things to think about

Sometimes, as a teacher, we can feel very isolated from our colleagues, yet we don't have to feel that way. Think about ways in which you can share knowledge and work on making sure that you spend time with fellow teachers and aim to learn from them. This is a difficult proposition – your workload is likely to be heavy and so is theirs but there are strategies to do this, so try them out and think about ways of promoting a community of practice within your organisation.

In a nutshell

This feature covers the essentials of sharing your knowledge with others and will help you to think about applying it to your own practice. This resource can be photocopied and used as a revision tool or a prompt for discussion with your peers.

The theory of action research

Lewin (1946) advocated the use of action research as a way of improving your own professional practice. This involves identifying an area of your teaching that you feel could be improved and then trying something new. Once you have put the new idea into practice you then reflect on how it went before making any modifications necessary and then experimenting again. The focus is on continuous improvement and so the underpinning idea is that action research is a cyclical approach that goes through repeated stages as illustrated below.

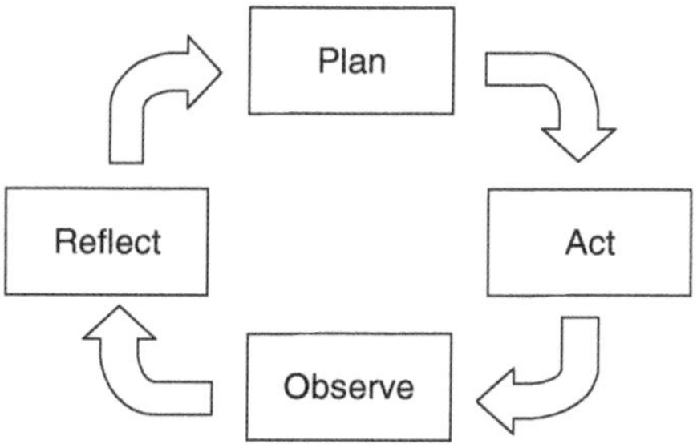

Source: Lewin (1946).

Putting it into practice

PLANNING
Firstly, identify an area of your professional practice that you would like to research. This could be something that you feel could be improved or alternatively it could be something new that you have to teach.

ACTING
Put together a plan for your chosen area. Think about how to improve the selected area and think about how you are going to measure the impact.

OBSERVING
Put in place the plan and see how it alters your teaching (this may be a positive or a negative change).

REFLECTING
Think about how the action research went – did it make a positive impact or negative impact?

STARTING AGAIN
Start the cycle again by making further improvements and seeing how they alter your professional practice.

Suggestions for further reading

McNiff, J (2001) *Action Research: Principles and Practice*. Abingdon: Routledge.

References

Department for Education (2011) *Qualified Teacher Standards*. London: Crown copyright, available from **https://www.gov.uk/government/publications/teachers-Standards** (accessed 6 June 2017).

Korzybski, A (1958) *Science and Sanity*, 4th edn. Baltimore, MD: Institute of General Semantics.

Lave, J and Wenger, E (1991) *Situated Learning: Legitimate Peripheral Participation*. Cambridge: Cambridge University Press.

Lewin, K (1946) 'Action research and minority problems', *Journal of Social Issues*, 2 (4): 34–46.

Wenger, E and Snyder, W (2000) 'Communities of practice: the organisational frontier', *Harvard Business Review*, 78 (1): 139–45.

Wenger, E, McDermott, R and Snyder, W (2002) *Cultivating Communities of Practice: A Guide to Managing Knowledge*. Boston: Harvard Business School Press.

18

Getting your first job

In this chapter we will explore:

- **when and how to apply for your first job;**
- **the application process;**
- **the 'golden rules' of interviews.**

Introduction

When you are in the middle of your teacher training year, it is very easy to forget about anything that comes afterwards but getting your first job is a rite of passage that can get your teaching career off to a flying start. It is an exciting time for you and the good news is that, for the past few years, demand for new teachers in many parts of the country has exceeded supply so the majority of teachers are offered a job before the end of their course. The temptation, of course, is to apply for the first job you see but that can lead to you making a mistake. The recruitment process can be complex and you should think about your options at every stage. The right first job for you is something that you need to think hard about and the purpose of this chapter is to get you ready for this decision.

Applying for your first job

During your teacher training it is likely that you will have been exposed to a number of different environments that will help you make your final decision about which job is right for you. For those of you in compulsory education, you would have completed placements in at least two contrasting organisations while those of you within post-compulsory education would have seen a great variety of teaching styles and locations to suit the needs of the wide range of subjects and students in this phase.

The key thing to remember when thinking about your first job is that everyone's needs are different. Sometimes it is easy to think that an 'outstanding' school in an affluent area would be a better option than a school that people perceive as having a more challenging catchment area, yet that is not always the case. The pressures, demands and rewards in contrasting schools are often very different and so that is why it is very important to think about your needs before starting to apply for jobs.

Similar choices are needed within the post-compulsory education sector with choices to be made about whether your expertise is best suited to sixth form colleges, general FE colleges, pupil referral units, prison education, adult education or any one of the many other forms of education that exist in the sector.

Figure 18.1 Job interview

Reflection

The purpose of this reflective feature is to get you to think about what you are looking for in your first job. For example, do you need to consider location, subject area or level of challenge?

Some things you may have considered are:

- **Geography.** Do you want to stay in the local area or are you willing to travel further afield? If you rely on public transport to get to work, are there any areas that you would need to avoid? Maybe consider other options such as working abroad or whether you would prefer somewhere closer to home.

- **Subject.** The next step is to identify the subject that you are going to put forward as your main subject. For some of you that will be easy, for example teachers of mathematics rarely teach any other subject, but for other subjects the choice is more complicated. A teacher of Business Studies is often asked to teach related subjects (for example IT or Economics) and so it is a good idea to think about what you would be able to offer.
- **Education phase.** For some people this is an easy choice. Most primary trained teachers work in that phase, but for other people the choice is trickier. While completing your teacher training you might have particularly enjoyed one or more age group and this will help inform your choice. A word of warning though: never apply for a phase if you have not experienced it. It is very easy to make assumptions and, aside from the difficulty you will have in explaining your lack of experience, you might find that your initial thoughts were incorrect.
- **Challenges.** Another factor to be aware of is the challenges you will face in each organisation and whether they will suit you or not. A high-performing school in an affluent area might seem like a more attractive option at first glance but there will be pressure on you to maintain results. A school or college serving a poorer area will have different challenges with teachers and lecturers coping with a lack of money and a variety of social problems.
- **Part time or full time.** This decision might be one that you are not able to make but for some people working part time at the start of their career represents a good way of easing themselves into the profession. This is especially true in the post-compulsory sector and represents a way of reducing the pressure that you have in your first year as a qualified professional.

When to look for your first job

The majority of people try to make sure that they have a job by the end of their teacher training year so a good idea is to look out for things from Christmas onwards. Remember that most teachers are required to give a term's notice when leaving, so as a result, jobs for September will be advertised fairly early on.

Increasingly, jobs tend to be advertised online and so it is a good idea to set up an alert that will email you when jobs that meet your specification are posted. The *Times Educational Supplement* (either in print form every Friday or online at **tes.com**) is the longest established source of new jobs but do not neglect other sources of information. Schools and colleges will advertise vacancies on their own websites while other good sources include the *Guardian Education* supplement on Tuesday, **jobs.ac.uk** and also your own university's Twitter account.

What to look for in a job advert

By now you should have a clear idea about the type of job and the location of the job that you want. However, it is always a good idea to take a very close look at the job advertisement before applying to save disappointment later. Make sure that you are applying for a role that is suitable for a newly qualified teacher and check to see if it is a fixed-term contract or whether it is open ended. Other things to check are whether it is full time or proportional (often expressed as a decimal, so one where you teach half a standard timetable would be described as a 0.5 post) and also if there are any additional responsibilities attached to the job.

Figure 18.2 Job hunter

Activity

Select a job advertisement from one of the sources that are listed above. Make sure that it is a job that suits your skills.

Before looking at the advertisement in detail spend some time thinking about how you view your role and come up with a few words that describe your philosophical approach to teaching - what are your key values and beliefs and how do you see your role? When you have done this, set this to one side and look again at the advertisement.

Highlight the qualities requested in the advert and then separate them into personal and professional. Reflect on whether you match those qualities and also whether the words mentioned in the recruitment advertisement match those of your own beliefs. Remember that it is not about getting a job, it is about getting the right job, and if your belief structure does not match that of the organisation then you might struggle.

If there is a match then this would be a job that you might think about applying for.

The application process

When most schools and colleges were controlled by the local education authority, the application process was relatively straightforward. A common application form was used and a lot of the information could be transferred if more than one application was needed. Sadly, this is now no longer the case and so it is difficult to generalise about the processes although there are a few general rules which you should follow when applying.

The personal statement

There is an art to writing a personal statement for a teaching job and, once mastered, they should not take too long to complete. One golden rule is to make sure that you don't just use a generic statement for each application – make sure that each statement is tailored for the specific job and you reflect on the qualities the advertisement asks for.

The structure of the statement tends to be fairly standard so it is a good idea is to follow these steps:

- **The introduction.** Make sure that you give your reasons for wanting to teach at the school or college. Be specific and show that you have done your research – look at the organisation's website, Ofsted report and any other information you can find and convey your enthusiasm and motivation for the job. Remember not to write what you think they want to hear, write your real reasons: you want to be selected on who you are rather than who you pretend to be.
- **Knowledge and understanding.** The next section allows you to match your own knowledge and understanding to that of the person specification. As with any application process, it is vital to ensure that you cover all aspects of the person specification and it is also vital to show how you have matched each aspect, so make sure that you give lots of examples. As well as that, it is a good idea to include some comments showing your philosophy. Schools and colleges are looking for people who can work independently from early on, so show that you understand the role of the teacher and make sure that you give concise examples to illustrate this understanding.
- **About yourself.** Once you have addressed the key aspects of the job, make sure that you include information about yourself. A good idea is to outline your personal and professional qualities concisely and demonstrate how these link to working in education. Another part to include is to note whether you have any additional skills which could be useful either in the class or in extra-curricular activities – these could include speaking another language, sport, music or art.
- **Conclusion.** Do not forget to include a conclusion in your personal statement. Too many applicants end their statement abruptly and this disrupts the flow. Conclude in a way that will make the person reading the application want to interview you and make sure you say why you are an excellent candidate for the job.

Once you have written the personal statement, put it away for a day or two and then read it again. This makes it much easier to spot any errors or mistakes that might detract from the application. Make sure that you check all spelling and grammar and check on the flow of the statement. Reading it aloud helps you focus on what you have written and whether it flows in a satisfactory manner.

Figure 18.3 Yoga

Activity

Once you have read the previous section, go back to your original advertisement and go through the process of writing a personal statement for the job. When you have finished show it to someone who you feel will be constructively critical, discuss it and by the end of the process you should have a personal statement that you can use as a model in the future.

The golden rules of the interview process

The final section of this chapter provides a few golden rules to follow once you have heard that you have been called for interview.

1. **Contact the school or college to arrange a visit.** Schools tend to do this as a matter of course although it is more unusual in colleges. When you visit, make sure you ask lots of questions and listen to the answers. Get a feel for the organisation and picture yourself working there. Be honest with yourself, if you don't like the place when you visit, then think seriously about whether this is the right job for you.
2. **Prepare for the interview.** By that we don't just mean organise your micro-teach or presentation – instead learn everything you can about the organisation and be ready to ask questions.

Figure 18.4 Golden rules

3. **Show off your teaching skills when invited to do a micro-teach.** Read the brief carefully and prepare something that is interactive and innovative. Do not do too much teacher-talk but instead remember everything you have learnt about structuring active lessons – show off your great teaching skills!
4. **Be organised.** Plan your route to the interview before the day and aim to arrive early. That way you will be far more relaxed than if you turn up at the last minute. Make sure that you are appropriately dressed for the job and that you have all the materials you need if presenting anything. A good idea is to bring two memory sticks and paper copies of any presentations, just in case of any problems.
5. **Whatever the outcome, learn from the experience.** Education is a small world and the way you are in one interview is likely to impact on your next one. Thank everyone at the end of the day for their time and if you are unsuccessful then always ask for feedback. Sometimes the reasons behind not being chosen are minor and relate to something that you can change next time.

Finally . . . good luck with the job hunting and remember to focus on getting the RIGHT job for your needs.

Things to think about

The key message from this chapter is that job searching requires a great deal of thought and preparation. Before applying, it is important that you are clear in your head as to what sort of job you want, where it would ideally be and what you will be teaching. Think about this early on in the course and start to plan. What steps can you put in place to ensure you take a structured approach to your job search?

In a nutshell

This feature covers the essentials of getting your first job and will help you to think about applying it to your own practice. This resource can be photocopied and used as a revision tool or a prompt for discussion with your peers.

Hattie and micro-teaching

Hattie's (2012) study of what works in teaching remains highly influential and one of the techniques he advocated was 'micro-teaching'. This is the name given to a short teaching session, normally designed to achieve a single objective. Many interviews will ask you to complete a micro-teach and it remains an excellent way of showing your teaching skills.

Hattie (2012) suggests that the key points of a good micro teach session are that the topic should be an interesting one, the objective clear and singular, active learning should be used and there should be time for reflection.

These points can be used as a guideline when designing a session. Using an andragogical approach (in other words, using knowledge that is already within the brains of students) can be highly beneficial and can help give students confidence to complete the task.

Knowing how much time is allocated is an important skill as one of the main problems for teachers is making sure that you fit everything in and avoid doing too much.

Putting it into practice

When designing your micro-teach think about the following:

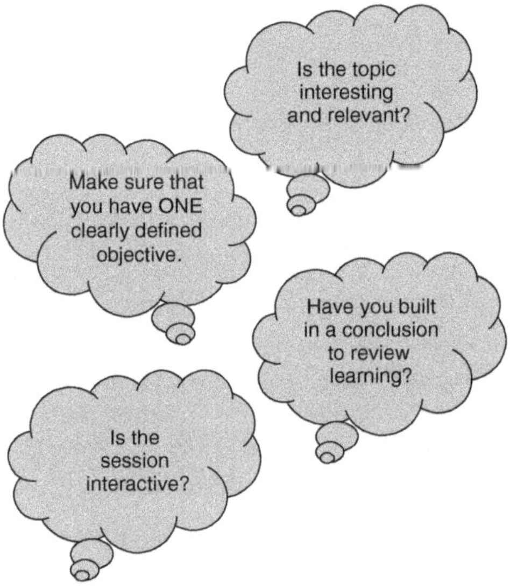

Suggestions for further reading

The best suggestion we can give you for further reading is to make sure that you read the *Times Educational Supplement* every week as well as the education pages in the *Guardian*.

References

Hattie, J (2012) *Visible Learning for Teachers*. Abingdon: Routledge.

19

The start of your professional journey

In this chapter we will explore:

- **making the most of your NQT year;**
- **taking control of your own continuous professional development;**
- **progressing within your career.**

Introduction

Starting your first teaching job is an exciting time and the first year can pass in a bit of a blur if you don't plan ahead and remember to take a look around from time to time.

This chapter is designed to help this process. It has been split into three separate sections and these represent the three stages of your career. The first stage is the newly qualified teacher (NQT) year: in effect this is when you are starting out in your career and will generally take you one year to complete (if you work part-time then it will take a little longer). It is your final hurdle to clear as you become a fully qualified teacher. The second stage looks at your professional development in the first few years of your career. This is when you are testing your wings, taking some risks and taking control to steer your career in the right direction for you. Finally, we will look at the slightly longer term – by now you will be flying high as your confidence builds and we will consider options for promotion.

Making the most of your NQT year

The newly qualified teacher year (normally abbreviated to NQT year) is a period of three terms which act as your induction into the profession in the compulsory education sector. It bridges the divide between your training and your career in teaching and is a great opportunity for you to learn more about the profession.

Figure 19.1 Career trajectory

After completing your teacher training qualification, you will need to complete the NQT year in order to gain fully qualified teacher status. This can be completed in any maintained school, independent school (including academies and free schools), nursery schools and even some independent schools overseas. The only thing to note is that you cannot complete it in any school that has received a 'Special Measures' judgement in its most recent Ofsted inspection. Once you have completed the year, you are free to practise in any maintained school as a fully qualified member of staff.

During your first year, you will be teaching a slightly reduced timetable (generally 90 per cent of a standard timetable) and will be supported if you are given additional non-teaching responsibilities. This means that you will have (a little) extra time to reflect and to complete the year. The year can be stressful, but there is always a lot of extra support available. A key part of this support is regular observations with a mentor who will be able to help you reflect on your learning and think about how to improve. This is an important part of the year as at the end of each term you will be assessed and targets will be set based on your progress.

You are only allowed one attempt at completing your first year and at the end of the year the head teacher will make a recommendation as to whether you pass or not. Remember that if you do not pass, you will not be able to practise as a qualified teacher in any maintained school so it is really important that if you have got any concerns about the process, you discuss them as soon as possible.

Within the post-compulsory education sector, the first year is treated in a rather different manner. There is no formal NQT procedure, but many organisations will have a probation year which runs along similar lines to the compulsory sector. There is no guarantee of a reduced timetable – this very much depends on the employing organisation – so that may add a level of stress initially. The same rules apply to this sector in terms of completing the initial probationary year so it is important to try to make the most of it and use every source of support you can to enable you to develop your professional practice. It is also important to note that the decision as to whether you receive the equivalent of QTS (QTLS – Qualified Teacher Learning and Skills) is not a recommendation from the organisation but it something you need to apply for through a separate organisation. Currently this is through the Education and Training Foundation which has a very informative website (**et-foundation.co.uk**) but please note that things change quickly in this phase of English education, so check with your tutors or mentor if you have any questions.

Figure 19.2 NQT

Activity

Reflecting on your own strengths and weaknesses is important for all teachers, especially new ones. It is easy, at the end of your teacher training year, to relax a little bit but rather than taking the whole summer off, spend time reflecting on your professional practice and before you start the year think about:

- things about the job that you believe you do well;
- things about the job that you believe you can do better;
- parts of the job that you will have to do that will be new to you.

Once you have thought about this, start to construct an action plan which will include sources of support and a timeline to help you put in place support for areas of weakness.

Surviving the NQT year – a five-point plan

You will be given lots of advice about how to survive your first year but the most important things are to keep working hard, keep reflecting on how you are doing and keep using all the sources of support available to you. In addition, this five-point plan might be useful to you.

Point one – learn how to say no!

Figure 19.3 Say no

Be very careful about any extra responsibilities that you take on at the start of your career. Your priority should be to pass the year and so anything else should not intrude on this. When you are in a new job, it is very easy to say yes to everything and although that will show how keen you are, it is very easy to become overloaded and unable to complete all the tasks that you have set yourself. This is where your plan that you completed in the earlier activity comes into its own – stick to it!

Point two – marking time

If you ask any teacher about the part of the job that takes the most time, and often causes the most stress, they will talk about the marking burden. Sometimes it feels relentless but it is vital that you stay on top of it and do not fall behind. We have talked in Chapter 2 about time management and making sure you have enough marking time is likely to be a key part of your time management. Allocate some dedicated time each day to marking and if you do feel as though you are struggling with this, ask others for tips on managing the load. There are some very good and very valid ways of getting students to peer mark and even self-mark some pieces that they complete, so if the process allows for this flexibility, it might be a consideration.

Point three – don't allow the job to take over

This is easier said than done but it is vital that you do not allow the job to become your entire life. Teaching is often seen as a vocation rather than a job and although it is important that you do the job to the best of your ability, it is very important to make sure that you have some time away from it all. Use your diary to block out 'me' time and do not neglect friends and family. It can be tempting to continue working, even when too tired, but it is far better to stop when you are tired, do something you enjoy and then come back to it. You will feel refreshed and be more productive.

Figure 19.4 Taking over

Point four – ask for help

You are not on your own in the school. Although it will sometimes feel as though everyone is madly rushing around in their own world, there are plenty of sources of support and it is important to use them. Everyone goes through ups and downs when teaching so there will be people who know exactly how you feel about the job and will be able to support you, offer advice or just listen while you talk through the problems you are facing.

Point five – celebrate successes

Whether it be your own successes or those of your students, make sure you celebrate what has been achieved. The feeling of pride when a student achieves something never leaves you as a teacher and it is important to make sure that you enjoy the good times. Consider putting up a success board or alternatively sharing good news in staff meetings.

Taking control of your continuous professional development

Developing as a professional is a vital skill to have and the lessons learnt during your teacher training can be used to good effect when deciding on your goals for your professional development. Sometimes there is a tendency to rely on the centrally organised days for support but it is often a good idea to ensure that you develop your own, personalised programme of CPD.

Figure 19.5 Celebrate success

One of the most important parts of any CPD programme is to identify the impact it has had on your professional practice. Sometimes this can be difficult to measure but it is a good idea to try as you will then see what works and what doesn't. The exercise below is designed to get you to think about the impact CPD can have and how you start to think about what difference it can make.

Reflection

Think about the following popular CPD activities and reflect on how you can tell if they have had any impact on your own teaching. This doesn't always have to be a change in quantifiable terms sometimes it could instead be intangible changes:

- a meeting to look at the new syllabus for your subject;
- a behaviour management seminar;
- a demonstration of new software designed to help with the teaching of a complex topic;
- a review of the homework policy.

You will find that there are a lot of CPD opportunities for teachers. Some of these will be internal to the school or college (known as INSET within compulsory education) while others will be external and either subject-specific or deal with generic topics. Finding the best CPD for you can be difficult but below are a few tips that will help you select what to aim for.

Make sure that the CPD will have a direct impact on your teaching

At the start of your career, your main focus should be on improving your professional practice and making sure that everything you do impacts on this. This means that you should look for CPD that will either improve areas you have for development or alternatively will help you solidify a strength. Look for testimonials from colleagues and ask if any materials will be provided that you can use.

Think about what you are looking to get out of the CPD

A key part of CPD is knowing what you want to get out of it – which isn't quite as simple as it seems! Initially it might be useful to use a model to structure your CPD like the one in Figure 19.6 below. This model has been adapted from Girvan *et al.* (2016) and is based on an experiential approach. The suggestion is that a starting point is to observe your learners as this will give an insight into the development need and the potential impact of it. This is followed by participating in the learning in order to get an 'insider view', something which allows you to experience what your learners will experience. This provides experience on which you can plan developments, think about how you might achieve them and finally refine your ideas into realistic actions. The model concludes with reflection on action to consider any further developments.

Figure 19.6 CPD

Sometimes one of the benefits of CPD is simply being away from your normal work environment as this can help refresh your mind and give you new ideas, but it is important to remember that useful CPD should have an impact, so have an objective and outline activities that will help you to achieve it.

All together now

Attending CPD events is a great way of meeting people and networking among fellow teachers. It is very easy to get into a set routine when you are teaching and meeting people who teach the same subject will often invigorate your teaching. Sometimes merely talking through the fact that you have the same problems within the classroom can help but in a lot of cases it is good to hear about different and innovative solutions to problems.

Follow-up after the event

Remember to see CPD as an ongoing process rather than a series of one-off events. When you get back to your school or college, try out what you have learnt from the training and see if it improves your professional practice. Don't lose touch with the people you have met either sharing good practice should be a lifelong process!

Activity

Put together a time chart for your CPD. This is an easy thing to do - all you need is a calendar and potential dates for activities. Each half term have one objective and select CPD that would help you achieve this objective. Add your school or college internal events and your chart will give you the complete picture of your annual CPD.

Progressing within your career

Finally, we will look at planning your career. The objective is to get you thinking about taking on more responsibilities. Many people are quite happy teaching classes and passing on their knowledge of the subject without taking on additional tasks, but should you want to, there are plenty of opportunities for career advancement within schools and colleges. Below we look at three possibilities.

Taking a management role

In all but the smallest organisations, there will be the opportunity to take on more responsibilities and perhaps advance your career within your subject. Most schools and colleges will have a designated person who acts as the head of subject and within this role it is often possible to guide the direction of the subject and put in place your ideas to improve teaching and learning. Within schools these roles will have a significant teaching load which makes it a busy job but keeps you in touch with what is happening in the classroom. On the other hand, in colleges it is often a non-teaching role which (in theory) gives you more time, but does mean that your connection with the classroom is broken.

From the role of head of department, it may be possible to expand your role and start to manage other areas. The majority of principals and head teachers started as teachers and worked their way up in this manner.

Taking a cross-organisational role

Within education organisations there will be a number of cross-organisational roles which might appeal to you. Some are likely to move you away from your subject (such as taking the role of SENCO – Special Educational Needs Coordinator) while others will allow you to continue to teach your specialised subject but will also let you share knowledge across the organisation (an example of this might be a head of teaching and learning).

These roles can be interesting, if challenging, and in most cases will require extra time studying which will be done alongside your teaching.

Taking a role outside your organisation

The other possibility is to take a role that takes you outside the organisation. Most subjects have professional bodies attached to them and a role within one of these can introduce you to new ideas. Researching and writing about your subject can also afford you a different perspective on the subject and, while all these roles do take time, they can be very rewarding.

Reflection

Think about what you would like to be doing in three, five and ten years' time. This is not an exact science but it will give you some idea as to how to manage your career. You might be happy being a class teacher for the duration of your career but if you do want to take on extra responsibilities then it is a good idea to think about it as early on in your career as possible.

Things to think about

Continuous professional development is a very individual process and is one that should constantly be in your mind. As you have been working through the previous chapters, we have been trying to get you to think about your own strengths, areas for development and also new areas for you to explore as a new teacher. One way of doing this is to keep a reflective journal – this will allow you to log your thoughts and ideas as you go along and will be something that you can look back on in the future for inspiration.

In a nutshell

This feature covers the essentials relating to the start of your professional journey and will help you to think about applying it to your own practice. This resource can be photocopied and used as a revision tool or a prompt for discussion with your peers.

Models of CPD

A key part of CPD is understanding what you want to get out of it. The following model (adapted from Girvan *et al.* 2016) suggests a starting point of observation of learners, followed by participation (in order to 'live' the learning experience), then planning, developing and refining ideas for action. This model concludes with reflection on action to consider any further developments.

Source: Girvan *et al.* (2016).

Putting it into practice

Identify a CPD course that you are going to attend in the near future, then go through the steps below:

1. Identify the objectives that you are trying to achieve.
2. Go on the course and try out the techniques or resources that you are going to be using. Think about it from the perspective of the student – what are the strengths, weaknesses, problems?
3. Apply the CPD lessons in your own classroom and see how it works. Remember to get feedback as you go along.
4. Reflect on the success (or otherwise) of the CPD.
5. Refer back to the original objective to see if it has been achieved.

If this works for you, use the same approach in the future.

Suggestions for further reading

Cowley, S (2013) *How to Survive Your First Year in Teaching*, 3rd edn. London: Bloomsbury.

Craft, A (2000) *Continuing Professional Development: A Practical Guide for Teachers and Schools*, 2nd edn (Educational Management). Abingdon: Routledge.

References

Craft, A. (2000) *Continuing Professional Development: A Practice Guide for Teachers and Schools*, 2nd Ed. (Educational Management). Abingdon: Routledge.

Girvan, C, Conneely, C and Tangney, B (2016) 'Extending experiential learning in teacher professional development', *Teacher and Teacher Education*, 58: 129–39.

20

A teacher's life

In this chapter we will explore:

- **the importance of attitude;**
- **modelling excellence;**
- **thinking like a teacher.**

Introduction

Look at the picture below. What do you see?

Figure 20.1 Pessimist

For some people, it might simply be a glass of water, others might see something that could act as a representation of a concept while others will vacillate between seeing the positive (the glass is half full) and the negative (the glass is half empty). In many ways, this illustration is representative of much of the life of the teacher: our 'glasses' are rarely filled to exactly the right level, but how we see this and how we subsequently approach our work will not only impact on our self-efficacy but also on all the people we interact with. As you progress with your career, there are a number of things that you can do to help you not only survive, but also thrive in the profession. In this chapter we will explore the ways in which your approach and the professional values and traits you develop as a result of this can help you to make a success of your new career.

The importance of attitude

Reflection

Think about a group you enjoy teaching and imagine yourself feeling relaxed and comfortable within your role. Your most recent lesson with this group went very well and you really feel as if you are making progress with them. At the start of the lesson, one of the students causes a minor disruption but you take it in your stride and move on with the lesson.

Now reverse your mood - imagine that the minor disruption had been in a class you didn't enjoy teaching and you had actually been dreading the lesson because you weren't comfortable with the group and felt you were making limited progress with them. Would you have responded in a different way?

The likelihood is that the minor disruption would have exacerbated your mood and the lesson would have been dragged down because of it. It is also very likely that minor disruptions will continue to be a part of day-to-day life as a teacher. If this is the case, consider what you could do in order to keep such disruptions in the category of 'minor', thereby ensuring that they do not envelop all other activities.

In Chapter 7 we discussed the concept of self-efficacy and the impact this has on how we manage events and interactions. In that chapter, we were concerned with ways in which you could build your own resilience in preparation for teaching. In Chapter 1 we considered the impact of your beliefs, attitudes and values in relation to how you carry out your teaching role with a focus on establishing the professional approach which will work for you as an individual. In other chapters, we have considered the impact of mindset, stress and the way you work with others, alongside a range of theories about how we learn and how we can teach. All of these things should provide you with useful knowledge on skills on which to base your practice but we would like to add an important caveat to the previous chapters: *none of the information, skills, hints, tips and approaches are likely to work without the right attitude.*

In order to evolve into, and master, the teaching role it is important to focus on our perception of events and the approaches we take as a result of this. It could be said that it is our attitude to life and work which determines our reality and as a result the experiences we have and the opportunities

Figure 20.2 Dark cloud

that are made available to us. The things that govern our thoughts also impact on everyday activities as they structure how we perceive and navigate the world, thereby playing a genuine role in our experienced reality. But the concepts upon which we frame our perceptions are not always things we are aware of – in a sense they are stories we tell ourselves about what is happening to us. With that in mind, it is possible that we can frame experiences in a positive way just as easily as we can frame them in a negative one.

Hill (1937) described the importance of positive psychology, which refers to how improved self-efficacy can lead to a positive internal and external approach. Put simply, he argued that a positive (or optimistic) view of life leads to internal calmness and also external happiness, which makes us more able to deal with the problems that present themselves. Nowhere is this more true than in the classroom where even the best classes contain moments of disruption or low-level problems which can be enhanced or diminished by our approach to them.

The problem with negativity

You may consider it appropriate, or even healthy, to verbalise your negative thoughts – indeed in some quarters it would be considered incongruent not to do so. However, it is important to remember that within your professional role you will have a significant impact on others and what you say and do will influence how others view you. According to Newberg and Waldman (2013) the expression of negativity can actually increase negative feelings which in turn disrupts our ability to properly evaluate and respond to social situations, stops us from making rational choices and encourages prejudice towards others (Newberg and Waldman, 2013), all things we might want to avoid in our professional and personal life. Although the suggestion is that expressing anger can be destructive, it is also acknowledged that repression of negative thoughts can equally have a harmful impact and that the best way to deal with these is to observe them inwardly without any judgement, then take steps to reframe the feelings in a positive way. Fredrikson (2009) suggests that we should generate three to five positive thoughts in response to every negative reaction we have. One way of doing this practically would be through the use of a reflective journal as outlined in Chapter 4.

Activity

Write down two negative thoughts or experiences that occurred over the last week. These could be thoughts about yourself or others such as *'I am not good at ... '* or *'Class 3B are impossible to teach.'*

For each of the 'negatives' write a minimum of three positives to try to reframe your current thinking.

Strategies for developing a positive outlook

Sometimes it isn't easy to be positive and, realistically, who among us can really say they feel positive all the time? Although we may have a tendency towards optimistic or pessimistic thinking, this is often a result of the way we have perceived and remembered our experiences – it is our own reality rather than The Reality. But research suggests (Fredrikson, 2009) that we can learn to be more positive and the following 'top five tips' may provide a starting point.

1. **Express appreciation.** You can do this by talking about positive events in your life and by expressing positive things about other people. It is important that these are genuine comments – most people can see through insincerity and mindless flattery.

2. **Recognise and refine your communication style.** Do you have particular habits in your conversational style? Is there a tendency to offload whatever is on your mind? Or point out all of your concerns? Do you listen as much as you speak? Recognise the limitations of your current communication style and interrupt any habits which are not aiding mutual communication.

3. **Think before you speak.** Speaking without any censorship can lead to problems both in the workplace and at home, so it is important to think about the impact of your communication. In Chapter 6 we introduced NLP prepositions and asked you to consider how these might impact on your current beliefs. Two of these have a very direct relationship to communication: *you cannot not communicate* which refers to the range of ways in which we give messages about ourselves to others. The second is *the meaning of a communication is the response you get,* which emphasises the importance of considering the impact of your words and your communication style and thinking about what you want to say before you say it. Imagine you are in a meeting and you strongly disagree with a proposal. Without censorship, you might say 'That's a stupid idea . . . '; alternatively, you could show appreciation and lead the thinking in a different direction with 'I understand what you are thinking but I think there might be a better way . . .'

4. **Consider the power of positive words.** It is true that words have enormous power to attract or distract, to stimulate the imagination, to create associations and to build or destroy relationships. When we use words effectively we can exert influence and are more likely to get what we want. A quick search on the internet will introduce you to lots of interesting sites which outline the most powerful words in the English language (often these are linked to sales and marketing) and while we don't necessarily advocate a totally rehearsed approach to communication, we would suggest giving thought to the image created by the words you choose.

5. **Look for the positives.** This was put succinctly in the following quote which is usually attributed to Winston Churchill: *A pessimist sees the difficulty at every opportunity; an optimist sees the opportunity in every difficulty.* By using techniques such as reframing it may be possible to see the positive in the most difficult situations. However, even when it seems difficult to recognise positives, it is always possible to take a pragmatic approach which ensures that you are in control of events rather than a victim of them.

Activity

The following list was presented on a website about positive leadership. Think about each of the sentences and consider why they might have a positive impact.

12 sentences to improve your communication:

I totally understand

Tell me more about that ...

What do you think?

What I hear you saying is ...

You're right

I trust your judgement

I don't know

Thanks

I'm on to it

How can we make this happen?

Let me play devil's advocate ...

I've got your back!

(Intelligence HQ.com online)

Congruence

The previous activity was intended to get you thinking about how you use language and the impact this has on others. Much of this information is useful in helping to take a more positive approach to your professional life; however, it is also important to remember the importance of congruence.

Figure 20.3 Congruence

Congruence refers to aspects of harmony and agreement and in this context could also be seen as genuineness, meaning that your communication should also reflect who you are. Being more positive in the way you communicate does not mean you should indulge in insincere flattery or say things you don't mean in order to appear more positive. It simply means you should think about what you say and the impact of your words. In the same way that certain words and phrases are intended to

Figure 20.4 Amazzzing

create a more positive image, it is also possible to give the impression of being disingenuous if your words appear insincere. According to Newberg and Waldman (2013) there are certain words which can lead others to think they are being deceived – a few examples are given in Figure 20.4.

There is a sense of irony in the fact that these words are intended to portray positive emotions and we are probably guilty of using many of them on a frequent basis. On reflection, their impact may have more to do with how the words are used rather than the words themselves. It is very easy, for example, to describe something as 'great' when you simply want to acknowledge it, but on its own the word doesn't really tell us anything – what is great about the thing or person you mention? If we are being congruent, is it enough to say: *'Fiona is amazing . . .'* or would it be more useful to say *'Fiona's use of questioning is amazing, she really gets the whole group to participate.'* We can assume you don't necessarily find everything about Fiona to be amazing, so being more specific immediately makes your words more meaningful.

Modelling excellence

The approach we have recommended in this chapter may, at first glance, seem like some sort of trickery aimed at fooling others about your positive outlook. However, there are very tangible reasons why your manner has an impact on your professional life. The very objective 'reality' of

Figure 20.5 Thought behaviour impact

day-to-day experiences may sometimes cause us to feel less positive but it is our subjective experience that shapes how we cope with these events. Subjective experience is what goes on in our minds as we interact with the world and the subsequent actions we take in life. Simply put, how we think affects what we do and the impact we have.

So how do you begin the process of thinking and behaving in ways which will ensure success in the teaching role? One of the most practical answers to this is by modelling excellence.

We all have the potential to achieve excellence in some areas of our life but we don't always know what 'excellent' looks like and as a result limit our own potential.

Activity

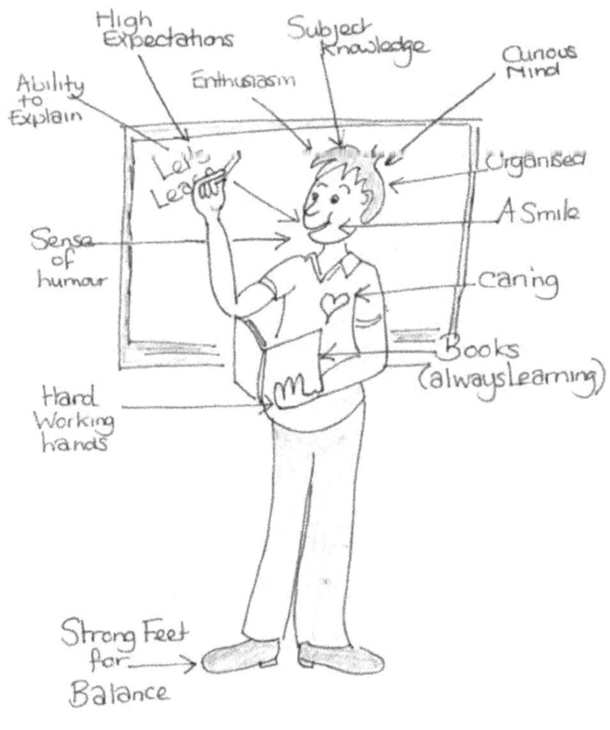

Figure 20.6 Excellent teacher

What does an excellent teacher look like? Write or draw your image of this person, making sure you highlight the specific characteristics which make up excellence.

In Chapter 12 we discussed social learning theory and the impact of modelling desired behaviours in learning (Bandura, 1977). In this context, we were exploring the ways in which interaction with others influences our learning. In this chapter, we are recommending a much more deliberate approach to modelling in order to develop skills in specific areas by observing excellence in others and adopting relevant strategies. This could be described as drawing on the thinking and behavioural strategies of others in a very structured way. The process of modelling excellence is based on NLP (neuro-linguistic programming) which was introduced in Chapter 6. According to the founders of NLP, Richard Bandler and John Grinder, a key focus is to make explicit the differences between someone is who excellent at a particular skill and someone who is not. The aim of this process is to study the patterns and structure of how a particular activity is carried out in order to replicate the language, thoughts and behaviours associated with the activity (Bandler and Grinder, 1975).

Reflection

Imagine you have to put together a piece of flatpacked furniture - what do you do? One option would be to unpack your item and try to work out what goes where; another might be to seek out information on the various parts that make up the piece of furniture, the ways these fit together and the structure of the overall piece so that you have a pattern to follow to build your furniture safely and effectively. Which is likely to have positive rather than negative consequences?

Just like the example above, most things have a structure. We all have strategies that work for us in certain situations and strategies we use in order to get the results we want. Part of your journey through teacher training has been about reflecting on what does and doesn't work and building your professional expertise around these things, but how do you improve your skill even more? The answer to this lies in modelling.

Activity

Think back to the activity where you described an excellent teacher and remind yourself of the skills embodied in this character. Write a list of the specific skills you would like to adopt (select two or three for starters), then think about all the people you know who seem to demonstrate these skills effortlessly. The list could include colleagues, mentors, tutors or peers. Choose one or more of these people and match them to the skills you have selected.

The process of modelling involves taking a structured approach to learning and adopting specific skills and can be adopted by using this ten-step plan:

1. Having selected appropriate skills you want to adopt and the 'models' which exhibit these skills, make contact with the relevant person/people and arrange to observe them doing whatever it is they do well.
2. During the observation try to locate a sequence of events; for example, first they observe the group, then ask a general question, followed by a specific question, followed by . . . and so on until you feel confident you have noted every step.
3. Write down any questions you want to ask about what you have observed, for example how do you know when to do this? What happens first? What happens next? How do you know that you have finished? Why do you do . . .? Or . . .?

4. Is there a reason for . . .? There may be things the model isn't even aware of so it is really important to list all of your questions.
5. After you have observed and then met with your model to reflect on your questions, rewrite the sequence of events you outlined in step two.
6. Arrange another observation of the model so that you can check and amend the sequence of events.
7. Picture yourself carrying out the sequence. Try to disassociate yourself and simply observe what you do as if you were looking from the outside in.
8. Imagine yourself following the sequence, this time fully associated. What do you think as you work though? How do you feel? What specifically do you notice?
9. Carry out the sequence for real. Don't think about it too much, just do it. Repeat the process as many times as you can.
10. Ask your model to observe you carrying out the sequence and provide feedback on what you do.

Use the feedback to refine the sequence.

Modelling is not a magic process and the whole process will take time, but by taking a structured approach you will learn and be able to improve your practice as a result.

Thinking like a teacher

The process of 'thinking like a teacher' is not one that happens overnight. Instead it requires reflection and effort and is something that tends to evolve over time. It is also difficult to quantify as it is something that feels 'normal' to those who practise it. In our experience, there are four key components that contribute to thinking like a teacher.

The first component is to adapt your approach to guiding rather than teaching. This is based on the work of Alison King, who suggested that the most effective approach to supporting individual learners was to move from *the sage on the stage to the guide on the side* (King, 1993). At any given time, you might have 30 students in front of you, each of whom has a different view of the world which influences how they understand and participate in the lesson. The only view you will fully understand is your own, therefore you must be the person to provide a palatable guide to support each of the students.

Secondly it is important to remember that you are one of the most consistent role models your students will see, therefore your approach to things will influence how the students view them. This can be influenced by how you introduce particular subjects or topics as well as how you deal with day-to-day activities. If you approach a subject with limited enthusiasm, this will certainly impact on how your students view it so it is important to ensure that your own particular views do not influence the class in a negative way. Instead, remember that you have the ability to inspire or extinguish your students' interest in a subject. Therefore a key part of thinking like a teacher is to develop strategies which allow you to present an enthusiastic representation of everything you teach (Sabik, 2015).

Figure 20.7 Thinking like a teacher

The third part of 'thinking like a teacher' is the ability to recognise when things need to change. In your teacher training – and indeed afterwards – it is very easy to see teaching as a science, in other words something where there are definite answers and definite ways of going about things. This manifests itself in tending to adopt a formula in the belief that this can ensure the success of the lesson. In many cases, having a sound structure is important, but teaching can also be seen as an art (Marzano, 2017) and this means that it is important that when things are not going to plan, you change things. At first this can be a worrying and disorientating experience. Rather than following an established path, teachers sometimes have to go 'off piste' and deviate from their lesson plans. Thinking like a teacher means that you learn to embrace the possibility that things might not work out, but remember – if they weren't working before, what do you have to lose by changing your approach?

The final characteristic is the development of a positive and resilient attitude. This has been the focus of much of this chapter and in many ways is the key attribute to develop. Students won't always be positive about your subject, they will misbehave and they will act in a way that you won't have predicted they will. You need to rise above it all, model a positive approach and ensure that you display the resilience that a teacher needs.

If you can combine these characteristics, after a while they will become second nature and you will behave in this way without having to think about it, once these behaviours have been engrained then you will truly be able to 'think like a teacher' and you will be ready for a long and successful career in this most rewarding of professions.

In a nutshell

This feature covers the key principles of modelling excellence in professional practice. This resource can be photocopied and used as a revision tool or a prompt for discussion with your peers.

Modelling excellence

The process of modelling excellence is based on the premise that excellent performance in any skill has a particular structure which can be replicated. Its simple aim is to make explicit the differences between excellent performance of a particular skill and mediocre performance.

Modelling is based on the principle that all activities are underpinned by:

- particular thinking – the why of the approach;
- certain methods – the how of the approach;
- structure – the order of events.

In order to model excellence, we need to generate an understanding of the why, how and structure by identifying specific patterns, behaviours and language used by the model. This provides a basis on which to replicate the skill, which is followed by testing and reworking our own application until we have a clear understanding of the skill.

This isn't a magic wand – it still takes practice, but the essence of success is in the very deliberate practice generated though modelling.

Putting it into practice – 10 steps

1 Select models and arrange to observe them in practice.

2 Create a detailed sequence of events.

3 Note questions to clarify specific thoughts, feelings and actions.

4 Reflect on questions and rewrite sequence.

5 Arrange another observation to check and refine sequence.

6 Picture yourself carrying out the sequence.

7 Imagine the sequence in a fully associated state.

8 Carry out the sequence for real.

9 Ask model to observe you carrying out the sequence.

10 Use feedback to refine the sequence.

Suggestions for further reading

Newberg, A and Waldman, MR (2013) *Words Can Change Your Brain: 12 Conversation Strategies to Build Trust, Resolve Conflict and Increase Intimacy*. New York: Plume.

References

Bandler, R and Grinder, J (1975) *The Structure of Magic 1: A Book about Language and Therapy*. Palo Alto, CA: Science and Behavior Books.

Bandura, A (1977) *Social Learning Theory*. Englewood Cliffs, NJ: Prentice Hall.

Fredrickson, BL (2009) *Positivity*. New York: Three Rivers Press.

Hill, N (1937) *Think and Grow Rich*. Greenwich, Greenwich, CT: Fawcett Crest.

https://www.intelligenthq.com/leadership/12-sentences-to-help-communication/ (accessed 9 August 2017).

King, A (1993) 'From sage on the stage to guide on the side', *College Teaching*, 41 (1): 30–5.

Marzano, R (2017) *The New Art and Science of Teaching*. New York: Solution Tree.

Newberg, A and Waldman, MR (2013) *Words Can Change Your Brain: 12 Conversation Strategies to Build Trust, Resolve Conflict and Increase Intimacy*. New York: Plume.

Sabik, C (2015) 'What does it mean to think like a teacher? Part 2', *Partnership for 21st Century Learning*, 2 (8).

Final thoughts

This book is intended as a guide to help you navigate the experience of initial teacher education by outlining the key aspects of the journey and to offer a map which provides some direction but does not stop you from discovering new approaches. It is our expectation that this will allow you truly to personalise the experience.

Whether you are fully aware of it or not, you will change as a result of this journey. You will gain many new skills and insights and you may even adopt very different ways of thinking. As we outlined in the Introduction, some of the things you learn will be fundamental to this change and you will recognise them as such; others may not yet have had a significant impact but they are important nonetheless.

That reminds us of a story. A group of travellers had been asked to collect pebbles, something they saw as pointless until the pebbles turned into diamonds. When reflecting on their experience, the travellers considered the difference between something they had considered worthless and then extremely valuable. This reflection, when applied in a wider sense, made them wonder how many other things in their lives that they had considered of little or no consequence might have a value that they hadn't yet discovered. As a result, . . . *they began to get more and more curious about discovering meanings under the surface of things, which only now were they beginning to comprehend* . . . (Hodgson, 2010: x).

You have completed the first part of your challenge and we now challenge you to continue to be curious and to continue to discover your own meanings. One journey is complete, the next is just about to begin. Enjoy!

Reference

Hodgson, D (2010) *Magic of Modern Metaphor: Walking with the Stars*. Carmarthen: Crown House.

Appendix

Overview of professional standards for english education

Primary AND Secondary	Post-compulsory	Relevant content	Chapter no./title
1. Set high expectations which inspire, motivate and challenge pupils • This includes creating a safe and stimulating learning environment, setting challenging goals and demonstrating consistently positive attitudes, values and behaviour.	**Prof Standard 3.** Inspire, motivate and raise aspirations of learners through enthusiasm and knowledge • Includes – conveying enthusiasm and using experience and knowledge of subject. Recognising learners' prior experience to tailor teaching. **Prof Standard 17.** Enable learners to share responsibility for their own learning and assessment, setting goals that stretch and challenge • Includes encouraging self-assessment, challenging minimum achievement and setting challenging goals.	**Chapter 12 - Teaching methods** **Chapter 12 - How students learn** **Chapter 13 - Modelling positive attitudes, values and behaviours** **Chapter 13 - Creating a safe environment** **Chapter 20 - Importance of positivity** **Chapter 20 - Modelling excellence**	**Chapter 12 - How Do We Learn? How Should We Teach?** **Chapter 13 - Creating a Positive Classroom** **Chapter 20 - A Teacher's Life**
2. Promote good progress and outcomes by pupils • This includes awareness of attainment and progress based on prior knowledge and emerging needs. Understanding how learning takes place and encouraging a responsible and conscientious attitude to work and study.	**Prof Standard 13.** Motivate and inspire learners to promote achievement and develop their skills to enable progression • Includes – identifying the strengths and weaknesses of individual learners, understanding links between subject and employment opportunities, using enthusiasm to motivate and help learners identify transferable skills.	**Chapter 16 - Egan's skilled help model** **Chapter 16 - GROW model**	**Chapter 16 - Pastoral Care**
3. Demonstrate good subject and curriculum knowledge • Includes own subject knowledge, critical understanding of curriculum area, promoting high standards of literacy and maths where appropriate.	**Prof Standard 7.** Maintain and update knowledge of your subject and/or vocational area • keeping updated on your subject/vocational area and collaborating with colleagues to expand your knowledge and understanding.	**Chapter 8 - Teacher competencies and teaching competencies** **Chapter 19 - Continuous professional development**	**Chapter 8 - What Do Teachers DO?** **Chapter 19 - The Start of Your Professional Journey**

Primary AND Secondary	Post-compulsory	Relevant content	Chapter no./title
	Prof Standard 16. Address the mathematics and English needs of learners and work creatively to overcome individual barriers to learning • Includes – identifying the needs of individual learners in maths and English, finding opportunities to develop these skills and developing your own skills.		
4. Plan and teach well-structured lessons • Means using lesson time effectively, promoting intellectual curiosity, setting out of class activities to consolidate/extend knowledge, reflect on lesson and contribute to curriculum planning.	**Prof Standard 4.** Be creative and innovative in selecting and adapting strategies to help learners to learn • Includes – finding effective ways of supporting learners and using technology to add value. **Prof Standard 1.** Reflect on what works best in your teaching and learning to meet the diverse needs of learners • Includes – critically appraising own practice and refining judgement on what works in own teaching context.	**Chapter 9 - Dispelling myths in planning** **Chapter 9 - What to include when planning** **Chapter 9 - Ordering a lesson and using Bloom's taxonomy** **Chapter 9 - Having high expectations** **Chapter 9 - Ensuring inclusivity**	**Chapter 9 - Planning Great Lessons**
5. Adapt teaching to respond to the strengths and needs of all pupils • This includes knowledge of differentiation strategies, understanding of barriers to learning, awareness of physical, social and intellectual development of learners and an understanding of	**Prof Standard 14.** Plan and deliver effective learning programmes for diverse groups or individuals in a safe and inclusive environment • Includes – promoting equality and diversity in your teaching and learning in order to create a positive inclusive learning environment, differentiating strategies to ensure all learners are involved, ensuring learning environment is safe and free of risks.	**Chapter 4 - Using reflective models** **Chapter 9 - Ensuring inclusivity** **Chapter 11 - Meeting the needs of all students** **Chapter 11 - Strategies to support students with special educational needs**	**Chapter 4 - Reflecting on Your Practice** **Chapter 9 - Planning Great Lessons** **Chapter 11 - The Inclusive Teacher**

(Continued)

Primary AND Secondary	Post-compulsory	Relevant content	Chapter no./title
specific needs including special educational needs, those with high ability, ESOL and disabilities.	**Prof Standard 5.** Value and promote social and cultural diversity, equality of opportunity and inclusion • Includes – promoting diversity within teaching and learning, highlighting different approaches and beliefs and seeking ways to overcome barriers to inclusion.		
6. Make accurate and productive use of assessment • Includes knowledge of assessment requirements, formative and summative assessments, ways of monitoring progress and giving feedback.	**Prof Standard 18.** Apply appropriate and fair methods of assessment and provide constructive and timely feedback to support progression and achievement. • Includes – understanding methods and application of assessments and the use of regular, constructive feedback. Understanding the theoretical and practical issues surrounding achievement from high-achieving to under-achieving learners.	**Chapter 10 - Only seven types of resources** **Chapter 11 - Supporting students with special educational needs** **Chapter 11 - Ensuring inclusivity** **Chapter 15 - Using innovative assessment methods** **Chapter 15 - Giving feedback and feedforward**	**Chapter 10 - Creating Teaching Resources** **Chapter 11 - The Inclusive Teacher** **Chapter 15 - Checking Learners' Progress**
7. Manage behaviour effectively to ensure a good and safe learning environment • This includes promoting good behaviour and managing classroom behaviour appropriately.	**Prof Standard 11.** Manage and promote positive learner behaviour • Includes – creating a positive learning environment; • Means – consider how the following can be used to help learners by creating a positive, proactive learning environment and being a role model for learners.	**Chapter 14 - Behaviour management** **Chapter 14 - Communicating in the classroom** **Chapter 14 - Using the intervention tariff**	**Chapter 14 - Effective Classroom Management**

Primary AND Secondary	Post-compulsory	Relevant content	Chapter no./title
8. Fulfil wider professional responsibilities • Includes contributing to wider role, developing professional relationships and understanding other areas of specialist support. Taking responsibility for own professional development and improving teaching.	**Prof Standard 2.** Evaluate and challenge your own practice, values and beliefs • Includes – regularly questioning professional values and beliefs, talking to colleagues, sharing insights, being proactive and managing own well-being. **Prof Standard 6.** Build positive and collaborative relationships with colleagues and learners • Includes – valuing teamwork and maintaining good professional relationships with colleagues. **Prof Standard 10.** Evaluate your practice with others and assess its impact on learning • Includes assessing own practice and working with others to improve it. **Prof Standard 12.** Understand the teaching and professional role and your responsibilities • Includes – awareness of role and responsibilities, keeping up to date, awareness of organisational requirements, local, national and statutory regulations, policy changes and legislation, curriculum, assessment and examination requirements.	**Chapter 1 - Values and beliefs in teaching** **Chapter 1 - Philosophies of education** **Chapter 2 - Self-assessment and understanding own strengths and weaknesses** **Chapter 2 - Managing time** **Chapter 8 - The role of a teacher** **Chapter 17 - Learning from others**	**Chapter 1 - Why Do You Want to Teach?** **Chapter 2 - Planning Your Journey Through Teacher Training** **Chapter 8 - What Do Teachers DO?** **Chapter 17 - Sharing Your Knowledge with Others**

(Continued)

Primary AND Secondary	Post-compulsory	Relevant content	Chapter no./title
No match in Primary and Secondary standards	**Prof Standard 8.** Maintain and update your knowledge of educational research to develop evidence-based practice • Includes – reading professional literature and reflecting on latest theories and research. **Prof Standard 9.** Apply theoretical understanding of effective practice in teaching, learning and assessment drawing on research and other evidence • Includes – using theoretical knowledge and engaging with research to improve practice. **Prof Standard 15.** Promote the benefits of technology and support learners in its use • Includes – keeping up to date, using technology to track progress and looking into ways of using technology to assist learning. **Prof Standard 19.** Maintain and update your teaching and training expertise and vocational skills through collaboration with employers • Includes – being aware of developments of teaching and in your subject/vocational area. Networking within professional communities. **Prof Standard 20.** Contribute to organisational development and quality improvement through collaboration with others • Includes – working with colleagues to improve systems, processes and policies, sharing ideas about best practice to improve quality.	**Chapter 3 – Working with colleagues and other professionals** **Chapter 5 – Using feedback and feedforward to improve your own professional practice** **Chapter 5 – Thriving on lesson observations** **Chapter 6 – Altering frames of reference** **Chapter 6 – Defeating the imposter syndrome** **Chapter 7 – Self-efficacy** **Chapter 7 – Emotional intelligence** **Chapter 10 – Creating ICT resources** **Chapter 17 – Peer observations** **Chapter 17 – Communities of practice** **Chapter 19 – Your NQT year**	**Chapter 3 – Working with Tutors and Mentors** **Chapter 5 – Using Feedback for Your Own Development** **Chapter 6 – Potential Barriers to Teaching** **Chapter 7 – The Resilient Teacher** **Chapter 10 – Creating Teaching Resources** **Chapter 17 – Sharing your Knowledge with Others** **Chapter 19 – The Start of Your Professional Journey**

Index